PANGAYAW AND DECOLONIZING RESISTANCE

Anarchism in the Philippines

Bas Umali

Pangayaw and Decolonizing Resistance: Anarchism in the Philippines
Edited by Gabriel Kuhn
This edition © 2020 PM Press

All images courtesy of Bas Umali and the Local Autonomous Network
(LAN).

ISBN: 978-1-62963-794-5 (print)
ISBN: 978-1-62963-819-5 (ebook)
Library of Congress Control Number: 2019946106

Cover by John Yates / www.stealworks.com
Interior design by briandesign

10 9 8 7 6 5 4 3 2 1

PM Press
PO Box 23912
Oakland, CA 94623
www.pmpress.org

Printed in the USA.

CONTENTS

INTRODUCTION

EDITOR'S PREFACE

The first time I met an anarchist from the Philippines was at Tokyo's Irregular Rhythm Asylum infoshop in 2006. Jong Pairez, an arts student, was living in Tokyo stocking supermarket shelves. For me, it was an introduction to labor migration in Asia. As we chatted with Japanese friends, Jong drew a portrait of me that I have kept to this day. It was not the meeting's only lasting outcome.

A couple of months after our meeting, associates of Jong's greeted me at Manila International Airport. They introduced me to the Philippine capital and put me up for a few days, before I found my own place to stay in the Malate district. My visit to the country lasted no longer than a month, but I was deeply impressed by the dedication and positivity of the anarchist activists I met.

The relevance of anarchist ideas for social movements in the Philippines was first presented to an international audience in Benedict Anderson's book *Under Three Flags: Anarchism and the Anti-Colonial Imagination* (2005). While Anderson focused on historical figures like José Rizal und Isabelo de los Reyes,[1] for contemporary anarchists in the Philippines other influences are at least as important, among them punk rock and the alterglobalization movement of the early 2000s. The latter helped establish horizontal forms of activism that allowed people to engage in social protests

without subscribing to the Marxist organizations that have long dominated the Philippine Left.

One evening in Malate, I met Bas Umali and a group of young punks. We sat down at a sidewalk café for a long chat. Bas, like many of today's anarchists in the Philippines, came of age in the Marxist milieu of the Communist Party and its affiliate organizations. Disillusioned by top-down organizing and authoritarian structures, he turned to grassroots alternatives and got involved in a variety of projects, from setting up radical publishing projects to establishing Food Not Bombs chapters. Our conversation with the young punks, whose names I sadly cannot recall, revolved mainly around the "Sagada 11," a group of punks who had been arrested after a festival in the highlands of Luzon. Accused of having been involved in a guerilla attack, they would remain in jail for a year before finally being acquitted.

After leaving the Philippines, I kept in touch with both Jong and Bas, and we soon conceived the idea of compiling a book about the anarchist movement in the country.

But publishing ambitions, especially collective ones, aren't always that easy to realize; you need to find the time, the right approach, a suitable infrastructure, and, last but not least, a publisher. We never got that far. But we collaborated on other writing projects, did fundraising together, and connected with people sharing similar ideas internationally. In 2012, German comrades organized a speaking tour by Cris, a close associate of Bas's and the founder of the Etniko Bandido infoshop in Pasig, Metro Manila.

We never fully dropped the book idea. Bas is a prolific writer. At the time we met, he had just finished the essay "Archipelagic Confederation: Advancing Genuine Citizens' Politics through Free Assemblies and Independent Structures from the Barangay and Communities." It can be found on various anarchist websites and was included in the third volume of Robert Graham's *Anarchism: A Documentary History of Libertarian Ideas* (2012). Other writings by Bas were published in different forums over the years. In 2019, Bas was looking for a publisher for a longer essay titled "Pangayaw:

Decolonizing Resistance in a Network of Communities in the Archipelago." When PM Press expressed interest, we discussed the possibility of adding material to it—and, almost fifteen years after we first discussed it, proceeded to compile the book we had thought about for so long.

It isn't exactly what we originally had in mind. The focus on one particular author hadn't been the plan, but you cannot always foresee the future. While no single voice can ever represent a movement, the texts collected in this volume provide an important entry point into the discussions and activities of contemporary anarchists in the archipelago we call the Philippines.

The fact that the author comes from the country it is about should not be noteworthy, but given the reality of international publishing it is. There are still many more English-language texts published *about* "non-Western" or "Third World" anarchism(s) than *by* "non-Western" or "Third World" authors.

It must not be forgotten, of course, that one reason for the international recognition that the anarchist movement in the Philippines receives is the use of English as a lingua franca. It is much easier to compile an English-language book with original writing from there than from Indonesia, China, or Egypt, although such books might be just as interesting and inspiring. This book is hopefully a step toward introducing voices that are heard much too rarely.

If these voices confuse Western anarchists, that is only healthy. You cannot stress the importance of non-Western forms of anarchism, while simultaneously rejecting everything that doesn't fit your idea of anarchism. Anarchism as a set of beliefs questioning all forms of authority is obviously attractive to many activists in the Global South. If their application of anarchism to the political and cultural realities they live in doesn't correspond with those of Western anarchists, it is time for the latter to expand their horizons rather than formulating critiques from their comfort zones.

In 2018, I asked Cris about his tour of Germany while working on an article about anarchism in the Philippines for the German magazine *iz3w*. He shared the following:

> For me, Europe is very privileged. This showed in the kind of struggles people were discussing: antifascism, critical whiteness, and other intellectual discourses, be it on labor or gender. Poverty, hunger, and basic rights are not frontline issues. People have more time to engage in intellectual and theoretical analysis compared to what we experience here. We need to think first and foremost about the practical aspects and benefits of each of our initiatives.

Bas Umali lives with his wife and three kids in Muntinlupa City, Metro Manila. After working for an NGO concerned with rainforest rehabilitation and being a Grab and Uber driver, Bas now provides technical assistance to marginalized fisherfolk. The projects he has been involved in over the past twenty years are numerous: zine publishing, organizing gatherings, setting up infoshops, managing programs, such as installing solar panels in poor neighborhoods and running solidarity campaigns that bring foods and medicines to typhoon-ravaged regions. The Mobile Anarchist School, established in 2011, takes educational materials to underprivileged communities.

When I talked to Cris in 2018, he had the following to say about the strength of the country's anarchist movement:

> I think the impact of the anarchists is still small. We are only a few committed individuals. But many people today question the sincerity of the so-called progressive bloc. Disillusioned leftists and freelance activists are increasingly engaging with independent political blocs like ours. People who formerly belonged to the authoritarian Left are now open to exploring other political philosophies. We are building new networks, with most of our allies coming from the arts scene and

environmental groups. We need to be careful not to be coopted by their movements, however.

A 2017 CNN Philippines article titled "The Anarchists Making a Difference in Philippine Society" confirms that anarchism in the Philippines is more than an insignificant fringe phenomenon. Bas is one of five anarchists portrayed in it, alongside Barbin, a University of the Philippines student, Fread de Mesa, a member of the Anabaptist-Mennonite Peace Church Philippines, Chuck Baclagon, who works for an environmental NGO, and Ron Solis, a "full-time anarchist" and volunteer. Portia Ladrido, the article's author, drew the following conclusion:

> For these anarchists, while they may come from different interest groups, they all form the same basic principles of "true" anarchism: that anarchism values the capacity of the individual to organize itself; that anarchism sees the role of the individual as a tool that contributes to a larger community; that anarchism is about mutual aid, directly helping any soul in need; and that anarchism is about the belief that humans are wired to pursue the common good, regardless of an authority figure.

It is no coincidence that only men are portrayed in the article. As in many other countries, the figureheads of the anarchist movement in the Philippines are predominantly male. Women, transgender people, and a new generation of

activists are increasingly challenging the patriarchal traits of the scene.

The introductory part of this book includes an interview that I conducted with Bas Umali and Jong Pairez for the German book *Von Jakarta bis Johannesburg: Anarchismus weltweit*

(From Jakarta to Johannesburg: Anarchism Worldwide, 2010),
as well as the article "Sketches of an Archipelagic Poetics of
Postcolonial Belonging" by Filipina Australian author Loma
Cuevas-Hewitt, first published in *Budhi: A Journal of Culture
and Ideas*.[2] The pieces provide important background information on the current anarchist movement in the Philippines
and place the writings by Bas Umali in their proper context.

The following texts by Bas were selected for this volume:

- "Archipelagic Confederation: Advancing Genuine Citizens'
  Politics through Free Assemblies and Independent
  Structures from the Barangay and Communities," first
  published on anarkismo.net in 2006.
- "A Pathology in Our Filipino Identity: A Disease That
  Decayed the Archipelago's Freedom and Prosperity," first
  published under the title "Three Stars in a Sun" in the
  journal *Gasera* no. 1 (2011).
- "Reconnecting Traditional Links: A Contribution to
  Understanding the Sabah Crisis," first published as a
  zine in 2013.
- "Dialectical Historical Materialism: An Effective Tool for
  Authoritarian Politics, Dominance, and Control in the
  Archipelago," first published on alpineanarchist.org in
  2017.
- "Pangayaw: Decolonizing Resistance in a Network of
  Communities in the Archipelago," written in 2019 and
  first published here.

All of Bas's texts have been edited for this volume.

Gabriel Kuhn, January 2020

NOTES

1 José Rizal (1861–1896) was a key figure in the late-nineteenth-cen-
   tury anti-colonial movement that led to the independence of the
   Philippines in 1898. He was executed by the Spanish authorities and
   is considered a national hero. Isabelo de los Reyes (1864–1938) was a
   prominent labor organizer.

2   The article was published under the name "Marco Cuevas-Hewitt";
     since then, the author has changed their name to Loma to reflect
     their gender identity.

ANARCHISM IN THE PHILIPPINES

Interview with Jong Pairez and Bas Umali

In the last decade, a remarkably strong anarchist movement seems to have developed in the Philippines. Can you give us a short overview?

Jong: There have been many published writings recently about anarchism in the Philippines, most of which are reflections, as well as prospects toward an alternative form of struggle and organizing that veers away from the traditions of the dominant Philippine Left. I can mention Bas Umali's "Archipelagic Confederation" and Marco Cuevas-Hewitt's "Sketches of an Archipelagic Poetics of Postcolonial Belonging." Both articles look toward the importance of diversity and decentralized horizontal politics commonly overlooked by a Left that is united with the government in the aim to build a unified nation-state. As Marco argues, "Nationalism in this sense might even be considered as a kind of 'internal imperialism.'"[1]

However, amazing theories are not always coherent in praxis. What I mean is that a movement capable of transmitting an anarchist mindset within various sectors of Philippine society is still in its infant stage. There are plenty of shortcomings to accept and consider. But, on the other hand, I see the shortcomings as a positive advantage for the emerging anarchist movement, because it provides us chances to creatively experiment and learn from mistakes.

Are there any historical movements in the Philippines whose politics had, from your perspective, anarchist dimensions?
Jong: Compared to anarchist movements in Europe and East Asia, most especially in Japan, the Philippines has no history of modern anarchist traditions and struggle in the late nineteenth and early twentieth centuries.

In the nineteenth century and during the peak of the anticolonial struggle against Spain and American imperialism in the early twentieth century, all revolutionary groups were preoccupied with national liberation. But according to Benedict Anderson, the author of *Under Three Flags*, European anarchists had a huge impact on Filipino intellectuals who were students in Madrid. One of them, José Rizal, wrote novels that were important for the history of the Philippine revolution. In *El Filibusterismo* (1891),[2] the protagonist is reminiscent of Ravachol, the French anarchist known for avenging oppressed workers by bombing targets of the authorities. Rizal symbolically equated this with the desperation of the Filipino people and their desire to liberate themselves from colonialism.

But anarchist theory and praxis never did proliferate in that period as a legitimate revolutionary alternative to colonialism in the Philippines. In Japan, anarchism had sown its seeds during the Meiji and Taishō periods, when Japanese anarchists became instrumental in struggles against the war and the emperor, as well as in building militant unions. There were some such developments in the Philippines, but obviously there is a contextual difference between the Japanese and the Filipino experience. So there is a history of anti-authoritarian struggle in the Philippines, but it is weak.

Some pacified Filipino natives, especially the discontented *principalia* (noble) class, were imagining a nation-state independent from their colonizers, but many indigenous brothers and sisters were fighting to defend their egalitarian ways of living in the mountains and other parts of the archipelago. Quasi-religious insurrections in Philippine history can be linked to antiauthoritarian struggles due to their desire of preserving autonomy.

Bas: José Rizal's novel depicts the oppressive character of colonialism and suggests a solution to get rid of it. Where did he get the idea from that the entire colonial elite could be exterminated by igniting the nitroglycerine hidden in a lamp? Rizal's long stay in Europe had made him aware of the anarchists' "propaganda by the deed." At the same time, his campaign for education as one of the key components of the freedom struggle is similar to Ferrer and Spanish anarcho-syndicalism.

In 1901, Isabelo de los Reyes returned home from a Montjuic prison cell in Spain to face the new enemy that disembarked from the modern warships in Manila Bay. De los Reyes's frame of struggle was far different from the nationalists we know today as heroes. Firstly, his object of criticism was imperialism. He organized workers and the urban poor in Manila and attacked American corporations. He practiced what he had learned from anarchist cellmates like Ramon Sempau. The Unión Obrera Democrática (UOD), which he cofounded, was the first workers' union in the archipelago. Direct actions through creative picket lines and strikes launched by workers and communities, particularly in Manila's Tondo district, rocked the colonial government, its corporate partners, and the local elite.

It seems that in quite a lot of your work you try to relate anarchist ideas to traditional ways of social organizing on the Philippine islands. Can you tell us more about this?

Bas: In my view, since time immemorial, anarchism has been present in the archipelago; primitive communities from coastal to upland areas flourished and utilized autonomous and decentralized political patterns that facilitated the proliferation of highly diverse cultures and lifestyles.

Primitive social organizations evolved until social stratifications formed and became institutions. The archipelago

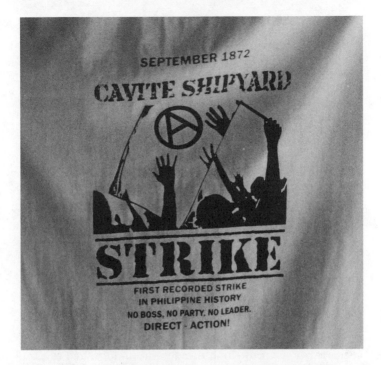

has various tribes with their own self-identity, culture, and sociopolitical organization. Before authoritarianism infected the revolutionary movement of the archipelago, direct action was practiced.

One example is the "Cavite mutiny" of February 20, 1872, when seven Spanish officers were killed in a mutiny at the Cavite naval shipyard. As a consequence, the Spanish authorities ordered the arrest of creoles, mestizos, secular priests, merchants, lawyers, and even some members of the colonial administration. In order to instill fear in the minds of the people, a kangaroo trial was held, and three secular priests were garroted in front of 40,000 people. Six months later, 1,200 workers went on strike, setting the first record in the history of the archipelago. Many people were arrested, but the administration failed to identify a leader and eventually everyone was released. General Izquierdo apparently concluded that "the International has spread its black wings to cast its nefarious shadow over the most remote lands."[3]

How did the traditional forms of social organization relate to the independence movement?

Bas: The Propaganda Movement was basically composed of the local educated elite.[4] They adopted the so-called Enlightenment framework from Europe. Giant names in history like those of Rizal, Emilio Aguinaldo, Emilio Jacinto, Andrés Bonifacio, Antonio Luna, Apolinario Mabini, and Marcelo del Pilar were all committed to nationalism as the basis of uniting the oppressed people.[5]

The elite successfully created the idea of an abstract large-scale community integrating highly diverse cultures. The culmination of the agitation of the Propaganda Movement was the establishment of the Katipunan organization that later formed the first government in the archipelago patterned after the nationalist framework of the West. Centralistic, coercive, and patriarchal institutions dominated social relations in the archipelago and undermined the traditional themes of mutual cooperation and diversity. Slavery existed in the form of the polo system.[6] Poverty and marginalization were introduced to communities that used to be prosperous and live in relative freedom.

Except for tribes and communities in the most remote areas, the entire archipelago became part of the regalian doctrine and Spanish hierarchy.

What can you tell us about the current anarchist movement in the Philippines?

Bas: Currently, broader nonhierarchical organization is limited to indigenous groups that effectively maintain traditional practices. Antiauthoritarian activism became dormant after the disintegration of the UOD. Yet anarchy is fairly strong in many places on Luzon, the Visayas, and Mindanao. The resilience of indigenous communities is related by their autonomous traditions. While they are forced to coexist with the state, they do not feel part of it.

Anarchy and antiauthoritarianism began to regain a certain momentum in the punk scene during the early 1980s. Punk's antiauthoritarian politics initially started as a critique of the conventional character of Philippine society. Soon, the punk and hardcore scene started to display antihierarchical politics and conscious anarchist propaganda. The movement attracted an increasing number of individuals, especially after the anti-WTO riots in Seattle ignited by the black bloc— the "propaganda by the deed" of our time.

Numerous collectives have formed since then in the National Capital Region (NCR), Davao, Cebu, Lucena, and other cities. They have conducted various activities, such as Food Not Bombs, community-based workshops, picket lines, discussion forums, publications, gigs, and graffiti.

Jong: Since the turn of the twenty-first century, activist groups and collectives that identify themselves as anarchist have been indeed sprouting like wild mushrooms in the Philippines. But, as Bas says, their background lies in the 1980s punk phenomenon, not in nineteenth-century anarchism. I would like to discuss this a bit more, given its importance for the present anarchist movement in the country.

The punk subculture came to the Philippine shores as a result of the Filipino diaspora. The beginnings can be attributed to rich teenage Filipinos returning to the country from Europe and the United States in the late 1970s. They were often referred to as *balikbayan*; *balik* means *to return*, and *bayan* is the *homeland*. Some of them brought punk rock with them, which was popularized by the DZRJ-810 AM "Rock of Manila" radio program. During this time, the military dictatorship of President Ferdinand Marcos was at its height. The media was controlled by the state, but a few small radio stations managed to operate outside of the state sanctions. Music by the likes of the Sex Pistols and The Clash stunned Manila listeners, and the "Pinoy punk" scene was born.

Once it had become popular, punk rock represented the dissatisfaction of the Filipino youth with conservative Philippine society. What, in the beginning, seemed like just another musical upheaval, very apolitical in nature, later developed into a radical challenge of authority. Youth into punk rock started to explore the politics of DIY and anarchism that were associated with it.

Unfortunately, the golden age of the punk rock scene in the Philippines coincided with punk's decline in the West, which had its ripple effects. Philippine mass media started embracing punk imagery, and it became instrumental to new marketing strategies by multinational companies.

Soft-drink giant Pepsi started sponsoring punk band contests on Philippine TV. This was still during the Marcos dictatorship. Several years later, after the dictatorship had been replaced by a democratic government under Corazon Aquino, Philippine mass media hyped up a satanic cult scare to discredit the punk scene, not least because it was a convenient way to cover up the Mendiola massacre.[7]

When other musical genres, such as new wave, hip-hop, and crossover, gained more influence, it created a divide between punks and others. Even within the punk scene, fragmentation became so rampant that groups would frequently clash over their musical preferences. It was a trend that echoed that of the Maoist Left.

The Left in the Philippines has often been characterized by severe infighting. Is this a problem in the anarchist movement as well?
Jong: The early 1990s are called the period of the "Great Leftist Split" due to the failure of the Communist Party of the Philippines to lead the overthrow of the Marcos dictatorship. The once strong and cohesive leftist movement was weakened by infighting among party cadres. There were even killings due to unsettled ideological differences about how to lead the people's uprising in EDSA.[8]

Unfortunately, fragmentation is among the shortcomings and mistakes of the emerging anarchist movement as well—petty claims about who is more anarchist than the other and so on. I hope that we can overcome this mistake by embracing our differences and being true to the idea of diversity. We must learn from the experiences of our indigenous brothers and sisters and leave the ghetto of punkdom.

The authoritarian Left has always been fairly strong in the Philippines. Why has the space for anarchist politics been limited despite the historical reference points that you have mentioned?

Bas: The influence of the authoritarian Left came to the archipelago after the disintegration of the UOD. From the UOD's remains, hierarchical organizations emerged, set to grab political power. The influence of Bolshevism facilitated this development. Later, Maoism dominated the revolutionary movement. From a semicolonial, semifeudal analysis of Philippine society, the Maoists set up a strategic people's war that was supposed to start in the countryside relying on the strength of the peasants.

During the Marcos years, the National Democratic Front (NDF) became the most influential bloc within the Left. It was directly influenced by the Communist Party of the Philippines (CPP) and reinforced by the party's growing armed wing, the New People's Army (NPA), which had been able to form battalions in many strategic regions of Luzon, the Visayas, and Mindanao.

The radicalism displayed by the authoritarian bloc attracted many sectors, including the youth, and this in substantial numbers. United against the fascists, the idea of a "popular front" gained influence.

The CPP-NPA-NDF alliance, whose primary means of grabbing political power was armed struggle, was pushed aside by the popular bloodless uprising that was successfully led by the elite opposition that installed the Aquino government. In the mid-1990s, the fragmentation of the leftist bloc commenced, and sometime later people started to point guns at one another. Various leftist political currents formed after the "Great Leftist Split." Some have been thriving in NGOs and civil society. But the most influential has been the "reaffirmist" one, maintaining the largest resources and the most active armed wing.[9]

We understand that you are involved in many efforts to connect anarchists throughout the Asia-Pacific region. How effective are your networking attempts and what promise do they hold?

Jong: The availability of new media technology like the internet can be helpful in achieving a defragmented form of organizing, which could result in a web of networks that will work for the advantage of furthering our cause. That is why we are working on ways to communicate our local struggles in Asia-Pacific and beyond.

What are your hopes for anarchist politics overall?

Bas: The ecology is critical to human survival and existence. During primitive times, natural resources were in perfect health and sustainably managed by local communities in the spirit of mutual cooperation and the recognition of diverse ways of life. One can always raise the population factor and say, "Well, the smaller the community, the less impact it has on the environment." One can also suggest that primitive technology was too limited to exploit our resources, and so on. Yet it is likely that it had much to do with the intention of the users of a particular natural habitat. If one's desire is to maintain and sustain the sociocultural needs of the local community, there is no need to overexploit natural resources.

Mainstream economy is designed to achieve infinite growth by increasing production and sales. But the very source of raw materials, essential for the entire global ecology, is finite and has defined limits. An economy that encourages massive extraction can only lead to massive exploitation of both natural resources and human labor. This means poverty of the many who have no control over the means of production and no access to the use of natural resources.

A few primitive people armed only with stones and sticks would have the ability to wipe out a herd of hoofed mammals. However, since these humans don't hunt to acquire wealth and property but to provide for the needs of their community, they will only kill the animals they need. Much of this is now out of balance. Take the example of a small community on an island highly dependent on fishing. It used its upland resources of trees to make boats. But since timber got a good price on the market, the community has now been enticed to harvest it all. As a result, the island's ecosystem and people's livelihoods are going to be destroyed.

In the archipelago, our ancestors did engage in local warfare and hostilities, but not to dominate others. They conducted raids, ambushes, and conventional warfare, but not to establish central power to rule the archipelago. Their conflicts were the result of unsettled debt, revenge, and unresolved territorial disputes.

Deriving wisdom from the autonomous politics and nonhierarchical social relations of our primitive communities is a process of recreating our own future social relations. The political exercises of our history proved nothing in terms of addressing critical issues, such as poverty, marginalization, slavery, and resource degradation. The experiences of the authoritarian Left in Vietnam, Cambodia, China, Cuba, Russia, Germany, North Korea, and other socialist states proved that the centralization of power will give special privileges only to the few who have access to power.

As human beings, we are part of an infinitely diverse global ecosystem; we are not above it. Creating a system that is advantageous only to a single stakeholder will only end up coercing. Anarchy is a social process in which people directly participate. Conscious efforts can lead to the establishment of systems that are designed to accommodate highly diverse interests, views, conceptions, and identities in a horizontal manner. Anarchy will seek to establish systems for mutual cooperation that facilitate voluntary processes of production, as well as the collective management of natural resources.

The establishment of a nonhierarchical society in tune with our ecosystem and free from poverty, coercion, slavery, and patriarchy is very hard to achieve. But it is an aspiration based on concrete experiences and practices of many communities around the globe.

It is unlikely that we will see such a society in our lifetime, as privileged groups will surely exhaust all possible means to maintain the status quo and to defend institutions that reinforce the centralization of power.

Education is the key to individual and social emancipation. Awareness about the state and other institutions that reinforce the centralization of power is essential in creating a new social order.

NOTES

All notes in this interview by the editor.

1   See page 11, note 2 about Cuevas-Hewitt's name change.
2   There are several English-language editions of the novel under varying titles, including *The Subversive* and *The Reign of Greed*; some English-language editions also left the original title untranslated.
3   Quoted in Benedict Anderson, *Under Three Flags: Anarchism and the Anti-Colonial Imagination* (London/New York: Verso, 2005), 58. Rafael Izquierdo (1820–1883) served as the governor general of the Philippines from 1871 to 1873. Known to be a ruthless ruler, he oversaw the execution of forty-one rebel soldiers after the Cavite mutiny had failed.
4   The term "Propaganda Movement" is used for the united efforts of artists, writers, and political organizers to fight Spanish colonial rule during the 1890s.
5   Emilio Aguinaldo (1869–1964) served as the first president of the Philippines from 1899 to 1901; Emilio Jacinto (1875–1899) was a prominent general in the Philippine resistance movement against colonial rule; Andrés Bonifacio (1863–1897) was a resistance movement leader executed by the Spanish; Antonio Luna (1866–1899) was a prominent figure in the Propaganda Movement and a military leader; Apolinario Mabini (1864–1903) was the first prime minister of the Philippines in 1899; Marcelo del Pilar (1850–1896) was one of the Philippine expatriates in Spain who, together with Rizal, instigated the Propaganda Movement.
6   Known as *polo y servicio*, a practice employed by Spanish colonizers for over 250 years that required the forced labor of all Filipino males from sixteen to sixty years old for forty-day periods.
7   The "Mendiola massacre" refers to the killing by security forces of a dozen unarmed participants at a 1987 farmers' protest on Mendiola Street in Manila.
8   "EDSA" refers to Epifanio de los Santos Avenue, where most of the demonstrations during the People Power Revolution took place.
9   The "reaffirmists" subscribe to a document presented by the Communist Party leadership in 1992, titled "Reaffirm Our Basic Principles and Carry the Revolution Forward."

SKETCHES OF AN ARCHIPELAGIC POETICS OF POSTCOLONIAL BELONGING

Marco Cuevas-Hewitt[1]

One of the great ironies of anti-imperialist movements in the Global South is that, despite their purported goal of liberating themselves from western cultural hegemony and political control, they arguably have yet to decolonise themselves of western imperialist logics; for example, those Enlightenment-derived logics pertaining to the transcendence of reason, the human, and the nation-state. The National Democratic Movement (NDM) in the Philippines is no exception. This is a revolutionary nationalist (and, more specifically, Marxist-Leninist-Maoist) movement, spearheaded by the Communist Party of the Philippines and its armed wing, the New People's Army. It has, from the Communist Party's founding in 1968 through to the present day, been engaged in continuous struggle against the liberal democratic Philippine state, seen as a puppet of Anglo-American imperialism. Being nationalist in character, the movement accepts the nation-state project as final and inevitable, with its notions of community and belonging therefore restricted within the premises of compartmentalised, national space. Its goal is to wrest control of the insular geography of the nation-state from the insular, albeit expansive, geography of empire. It resists imperial homogenisation across transnational space but replicates these homogenising imperatives within the bounds of the nation-state space it aims to liberate. Thus, despite resisting external domination, the NDM, like all revolutionary nationalist movements, contains powerful structures of *internal* domination. Nationalism, in this sense, might even be considered as a kind of "*internal imperialism.*" As Chua Beng Huat writes, Philippine nationalists did not erase Anglo-American imperialist ideology, "but rather 'Filipinized' it as part of their own nationalist ideology."[2] The modernist epistemology underpinning the NDM renders it largely intolerant of difference, reducing the multiplicity of cultural identities in the Philippines to a unity; that is, to a single, homogenous conception of what it means to be a "true" and "authentic" Filipino.

In effect, then, the Philippines, despite being an *archipelago*, is discursively rendered as mere *island*. Starting from the premise that revolutionary nationalism constitutes an anachronism in the current context, I will argue in this paper that there is an urgent need to refound struggle upon new imaginaries of social space. To these ends, I would like to propose the "archipelago" as an alternative imaginary to the centralising, homogenising, and essentialising schema of nation-state or "island" space. The new archipelagic poetics which I am proposing would valorise what John Tomlinson calls "complex connectivity," rather than homogenous "unity,"[3] allowing for commonalities to be constructed *across* differences, rather than at the expense of them. It would furthermore allow for notions of community and belonging to become refounded on *affinities* rather than essences, rendering the Philippines as a multiplicitous *translocal* community, rather than a unitary *national* one. Importantly, the various nodes of the Filipino diaspora might also be considered as part of the archipelago.

Before proceeding, however, it will be necessary to delve into a deeper discussion of that which I will be differentiating the archipelago from; that being the modernist conception of social space, for which I am employing the trope of the *island*.

Island Space and Its Discontents

In a recent article, the postcolonial literary theorist Antonis Balasopolous coined the term "nesology" to refer to the "discursive production of insularity," with the prefix "neso-" deriving from the Greek root for "island."[4] The descriptor, "nesological," then, is used figuratively by Balasopolous to speak of phenomena commonly rendered or perceived as bounded and insular; that is to say, *island-like*. The "bounded morphological schema of the island" becomes the analogue and archetype for all the circumscribed entities that populate the modernist imaginary;[5] for example, the individual, the body, the society, and so on. The nation-state is perhaps the example par excellence.

The nation-state-centric view of the world could, in fact, be seen as an extension of the "nesological" worldviews of Isaac Newton and Immanuel Kant, to whom much of modernist thought is indebted. Their vision is one of a stable universe composed of discrete, bounded entities. In effect, it sees only *islands of order*, at the same time forgetting that there is a whole *ocean* out there; an ocean that mixes the things of the world. It is blind to the chaos from which all actuality is generated, preoccupying itself instead with the imposition of order; that is, with a vain attempt at the taxonomisation and encoding of all reality. The Newtonian-Kantian ontology of order sees the world we are born into as always already mapped out in a series of contiguous, stable, a priori categories, in effect imposing a stark geometry of *inside* and *outside* upon thought. This, in turn, gives rise to an epistemically violent logic of "either-or," in which difference can only be conceived of in absolute terms.

Since nationalism invariably valorizes unity over multiplicity (in other words, island space over archipelagic space), it is simply unable to account for flux or heterogeneity, therefore marginalising or ignoring by default alternative forms of experience which overspill or evade the nationalist frame. The Philippines, then, despite being a rich site of cultural hybridity, is discursively naturalised as a unitary national community—one history, one people, one telos, and so on—by nationalist scholars. From this perspective, multiplicity and hybridity represent "pollution and impurity."[6] The liminal and the ambiguous are rendered as threatening, renegade elements that either need to become wholly, often forcibly, incorporated into the "inside" or else banished to the "outside." This is the same disastrous logic which led to the horrendous purges within the NDM in the late eighties.

Certainly, it must be admitted that modernist and, more specifically, nationalist, forms of belonging have undergone somewhat of a resurgence in recent times, which is, of course, seemingly at odds with many of the triumphalist assertions of early scholars of globalisation that the increasing integration of the world would automatically lead to more post-nationalist and cosmopolitan dispositions. Franco Berardi contends that the increased appeal of nationalism and other forms of absolutism in fact followed on from "the panic unleashed by the postmodern condition."[7] This is precisely because, from the perspective of the world that is being lost, postmodernity becomes associated with processes of social fragmentation and disintegration. If we shift our gaze, however, to the world that is being *made* (instead of just that which is being lost), postmodernity is soon able to become understood in terms of a more positive conception of "complex connectivity" (Tomlinson). It is not only that social relations are disintegrating, but also that they are changing and being reconstituted. Postmodernity, therefore, is not just about the "collapse of grand narratives"[8] but also about the fomentation of new subjectivities, the liberation of "subversive multiplicities,"[9] and the proliferation of innumerable micro-narratives that refuse conformity to all the old categories and constants of modernity.

Toward an Archipelagic Reconfiguration of Social Space

In a brief online article by Filipino anarchist writer Bas Umali, a startling proposition is made; one calling for the dismantling of the Philippine nation-state and the implementation of an "archipelagic confederation" in its place. Umali's vision is presented as a stateless, anarchist alternative to the state socialist goal of "National Democracy," as proposed by José Maria Sison, the founder of the Communist Party of the Philippines and principal theorist of the NDM. An archipelagic confederation would, in Umali's words, be "a structure that connects and interlinks politically and economically every community in the archipelago," without the need for a centralized state.[10] It would consist of networks of autonomous villages (barangays), together comprising regional assemblies in which translocal coordination could take place. These regional assemblies, in turn, would constitute an archipelago-wide assembly. Importantly, this vision balances local autonomy with regional solidarity and coordination. The local is not disregarded or deemed subservient to the national, as is the case with the nation-state. The goal is one of constructing heterogeneous *affinities* between autonomous localities, not one of enforcing homogenous conformity to a higher centralized authority.

Questions of whether or not it is at all possible to bring about an archipelagic confederation in practical terms are, for me, beside the point. Putting all such questions aside, what is most important about Umali's proposal is the very fact that such a postnationalist reimagining of social space has taken—and is taking—place. Umali's vision could perhaps be seen as symptomatic of some more profound mutations of subjectivity currently being engendered under conditions of postmodernity. In addition, it is a not insignificant fact that such a decentralized, network-oriented, and translocal reimagining of social space has emerged from the specifically *anarchist* milieu in the Philippines. Anarchism, as a current of radical political thought and practice, has, after all, always defined itself in opposition to centralized power and to the homogenous collectivities favoured by state socialist thought. It is also becoming an increasingly attractive option for radical young activists in the Philippines, who have understandably become disillusioned with the Maoist orthodoxy of the NDM, which for so long had enjoyed hegemonic status on the Philippine Left.

Following Umali, perhaps we can reclaim the term used to refer to the Philippines *before* it was constituted as a modern nation-state; that term being, simply, the "Philippine *archipelago*." According to Fijian anthropologist Epeli Hau'ofa, the precolonial world was one "in which people and cultures moved and mingled, unhindered by boundaries of the kind erected much later by imperial powers."[11] What he wrote of the South Pacific is also much the case with pre-colonial Philippines: "From one island to another they sailed to trade and to marry, thereby expanding social networks for greater flows of wealth."[12] These maritime flows have historically been of central importance in the constitution of cultural identities in the Philippines. This is evident in the fact that ethnolinguistic groups in the Philippine archipelago do not map with particular islands but, rather, with particular maritime regions. For example, the Cebuano language is spoken on the island of Cebu, as well as in the eastern portion of Negros and the western portion of Leyte, both of which face Cebu. As a further example, Waray is spoken on the island of Samar, as well as in Eastern Leyte, which faces Samar. Culture can therefore be seen to be produced in *flows*. Indeed, *no culture is an island*.

The sea, then, does not constitute a barrier but, rather, a connective tissue crossed by perpetual flows. The importance of the trope of the archipelago is exactly this; that it shifts attention *away* from compartmentalized island space and redirects our gaze toward the *relational* space of the sea. In this sense, the archipelago, as I conceive of it here, is *not* reducible to a mere aggregate of scattered territorial surfaces or a collection of individual islands. Instead, what is significant about the archipelago is the *sea between*—a site of a multiple series of relations that are never fixed but constantly in flux. The networked space of the archipelago which I am attempting to articulate here finds resonance in Stéphane Dufoix's notion of "atopic space," which he describes as "a space of more than a place, a geography with no other territory than the space described by the networks . . . a territory without terrain."[13] It is important to note here that the local is in no way erased by atopic or archipelagic space; it is just that it is seen as inextricably connected to and enriched by the translocal, itself enriching the translocal in turn.

The question I would like to pose at this point is: Would it at all be possible to find belonging or construct community in a "territory without terrain," as Dufoix puts it?[14] We have hitherto only been able to imagine belonging in terms of compartmentalized island space. Perhaps it is time to consider, instead, the possibility of making a home for ourselves in the archipelagic sea; that is to say, to construct new forms of belonging based on *affinities*, rather than essences. "Essences" are those attributes constituting a rigid, invariable ideal to which people must conform. Essence-based collectivities thus impose strict criteria for membership and are intolerant of difference. I use the term *affinity*, in contrast, to describe those social solidarities which ride, rather than erase, difference. A necessary recognition of the world and everything in it as irreducibly plural and multivalent, in fact, lies at the heart of the archipelagic poetics that I am proposing in this paper. An archipelagic poetics would resist any attempt to reduce a multiplicity to a unity. Homogenous unity should *not*, as is the case with nationalism, be considered a precondition for life in common, since it is entirely possible for commonalities or affinities to be constructed between different elements without necessarily effacing their heterogeneity. As Balasopoulos argues, we need to recognise "the simultaneous provenance of singularity and interconnectedness constituting the experience of the world."[15]

Significantly, in place of the modernist revolutionary projects of old (of which that of the NDM in the Philippines is a prime example), Michael Hardt and Antonio Negri articulate the possibility of a new revolutionary project; one centred around the concept of the "multitude." The multitude is described, simply, as "singularities that act in common."[16] Instead of the homogenizing notions of the nation or the working class, then, struggle is refounded on a radical plurality of agents, which are nevertheless able to forge a common project. Such is the case with the alternative globalisation movement today. There are also a number of other important examples which could be invoked. Third Wave feminism and the queer liberation movement, for instance, have been at the cutting edge of articulating and inventing a new postmodern politics of the sort that the concept of the "multitude" attempts to capture and describe. If we accept Jeffrey Juris' perspective of social movements as laboratories of alternative values and practices, then we cannot afford to ignore the nascent forms of subjectivity emerging from these milieux.[17] Alternative futures are indeed *prefigured* in the present. Queer identity perhaps serves as a perfect example of a multivalent identity, with plurality and flux inextricably structured into it from the beginning. There is no one way of being queer, and queer circles certainly do not require conformity to any a priori essences. On the contrary, *diversity is valued in its own right.* Such is the radical shift in thinking that an archipelagic poetics would hope to bring about.

Conclusion

I would like to propose, in conclusion, that the task of an archipelagic poetics in the current context would be to foment new, multivalent, *archipelagic* forms of identity and community, in ways which refuse and overspill the boundaries and terms of compartmentalized island space. Not only would it seek to spark new forms of sociality and ways of being in the world, but it would also attempt to make explicit that which is already implicit. As I conjectured earlier, perhaps Umali's vision of an archipelagic confederation is reflective of deeper mutations of subjectivity currently being engendered in the collective psyche through processes associated with postmodernity. An archipelagic poetics would grope toward a language better able to articulate the postcolonial present, for instance, favouring fluid, "seabound" metaphors and tropes over static, "earthbound" ones. As has been emphasised throughout this paper, it would also serve as a valuable and much-needed antidote to the "tragic popularity of ideas about the integrity and purity of cultures,"[18] aiming to undo the block to thought that is the nation, thereby opening up new possibilities for liberation.

NOTES

1   See page 11, note 2 about Cuevas-Hewitt's name change.—editor's note
2   Beng Huat Chua, "Southeast Asia in Postcolonial Studies: An Introduction," Postcolonial Studies 11, no. 3 (2008): 231–40.
3   John Tomlinson, Globalization and Culture (Cambridge: Polity Press, 1999).
4   Antonis Balasopolous, "Nesologies: Island Form and Postcolonial Geopoetics," Postcolonial Studies 11, no. 1 (2008): 9–26.
5   Ibid., 13.
6   Paul Gilroy, The Black Atlantic: Modernity and Double Consciousness (London: Verso, 1993), 2.
7   Franco Berardi, Felix Guattari: Thought, Friendship, and Visionary Cartography (New York: Palgrave Macmillan, 2008), 139.
8   Jean-François Lyotard, The Postmodern Condition: A Report on Knowledge (Minneapolis: University of Minnesota Press, 1984).
9   Judith Butler, Gender Trouble: Feminism and the Subversion of Identity (New York: Routledge, 1990).
10 Bas Umali, "Archipelagic Confederation: Advancing Genuine Citizens' Politics through Free Assemblies and Independent Structures from the Barangay and Communities," 2006, quoted from www.anarkismo.net/article/2923.
11 Epeli Hau'ofa, Our Sea of Islands. We Are the Ocean: Selected Works (Honolulu: University of Hawai'i Press, 2008), 33.
12 Ibid.
13 Stéphane Dufoix, Diasporas (Berkeley: University of California Press, 2008), 63.
14 Ibid.
15 Balasopoulos, "Nesologies," 18.
16 Michael Hardt and Antonio Negri, Multitude: War and Democracy in the Age of Empire (New York: Penguin Press, 2004), 105.
17 Jeffrey Juris, Networking Futures: The Movements against Corporate Globalization (Durham, NC: Duke University Press, 2008).
18 Gilroy, The Black Atlantic, 7.

TEXTS BY BAS UMALI

ARCHIPELAGIC CONFEDERATION

Advancing Genuine Citizens' Politics through Free Assemblies and Independent Structures from the Barangay and Communities (2006)

Introduction

Many of us will agree that in our context democracy seems elusive. A vast number of people are in extreme poverty, deprived of basic needs and politically marginalized. We know that poverty is caused by the uneven distribution of power, where only a few can decide over critical things, such as the use of natural resources and the distribution of their benefits. Who among us was ever asked or consulted by the government in its program of environmental destruction which has only profited big corporations controlled by a few families and foreign corporations? Did the government bother to ask peasants, farmers, fishers, workers, women, youth, gays, consumers, and other sectors with regard to the country's accession to the WTO and the signing of various bilateral agreements? Who wants E-VAT and debt payment?[1] The list is overwhelmingly long, proving that the democracy we have today is a farce.

The heart of the struggle of all the revolutionary efforts in our history is about making people participate in power. People's participation in decision-making is central, because without people's participation in the political exercises that directly influence every dimension of their lives, democracy will not be realized.

This document will attempt to discuss an alternative anarchist political structure that will promote people's direct participation in power and, in broad strokes, discuss the flow of political power from the bottom to the top. It is a concept that is heavily derived from the idea of a confederation advanced by libertarian author Murray Bookchin. This idea is not detached from traditional anarchist movements and contemporary anarchist activists; we believe it is highly relevant to our current political crisis.

A confederation offers an alternative political structure based on a libertarian framework, i.e., nonhierarchical and non-statist, which is doable and applicable. It is doable compared to the thirty-five-year-old struggle of the CPP-NPA-NDF,[2] which, after taking tens of thousands of lives, has not delivered any concrete economic and political output for the Filipino people. Moreover, the alternatives being proposed by mainstream leftist groups outside the NDF offer no substantial difference, for they all adhere to the state and to capturing political power—an objective that cannot be realized in the near future.

Considering that anarchism is exaggeratedly misunderstood, let us first discuss some fundamental principles of stateless socialism, libertarianism, and anarchism.

"Purely utopian!" That's one of the common reactions of those who do not understand the word *anarchy* and the alternatives it offers. Another misconception is its affinity to chaos. These nuisances and misinterpretations are not surprising at all. Historically, anarchism has long opposed oppressive systems and fought monarchy, oligarchy, and the totalitarianism of the state socialists and authoritarian communists alike. It continuous with the struggle to fight new forms of colonialism, capitalism, and other exploitative systems that hamper the development of humanity. Every ruling regime has its share in imputing fear and terror on the anarchist movement in order to discredit it.

It is impossible to escape the fact that violence is part of the anarchist movement. Along with nationalists and republicans, anarchists used terroristic methods to advance social revolution. The "propaganda by the deed" was meant to encourage people to act against the state and the old order by launching violent acts. There are various examples: Italian anarchist Sante Geronimo Caserio killed French president Marie François Sadi Carnot in 1894; his compatriot Michele Angiolillo shot the Spanish prime minister Antonio Cánovas in 1897; Luigi Lucheni, another anarchist from Italy, stabbed Empress Elisabeth of Austria to death in 1898; and Polish anarchist Leon Czogolsz killed US president William McKinley in 1901. There were also two attempts on the life of Kaiser Wilhelm I, the first by Max Hödel in May 1878, the second by Karl Nobiling just one month later. The list is long.

These incidents were used by the dominant regimes to their own advantage. In order to demonize anarchism, they shrewdly related it to violence and chaos. This was reinforced by the state socialists and authoritarian communists when the anarchist movement in Ukraine challenged the Bolshevik regime, the White Army, and other foreign invaders.

Nuisances and misinterpretations are bound to occur in situations where power is asymmetrically distributed. The political structure that is controlled by the economic and political elite will not allow anarchism to flourish. Moreover, the revolutionary tradition in the Philippines is highly influenced by red bureaucracy, which is historically hostile to anarchism.

Contrary to common misconceptions, anarchism is a theory that firmly upholds the idea of an organized world that is free for all. As Noam Chomsky once stated in an interview, anarchy is a society that is highly organized, with many different structures being integrated, such as the workplace, the community, and other myriad forms of free and voluntary associations, where participants directly manage their own affairs.

Unlike the existing order—in which people are motivated by power, profit, private property, and individualism—anarchy is a society that fosters mutual cooperation, solidarity, and freedom from exploitation and oppression. Decisions are made by those directly concerned. Any form of political structure that centralizes power is unacceptable.

The term *archipelago* recognizes the geographical characteristics of the country called the Philippines and the very essential role of its rich natural resources that strongly influence the lifestyle of its inhabitants. Myriad historical accounts indicate that the bodies of water surrounding the different islands actually connect rather than separate them from each other, and that the inhabitants' economic, social, and political activities were developed due to the interconnectedness of their immediate environment.

It is also important to note that the rich natural endowments of the archipelago allow diverse cultures to flourish and develop in heterogeneous ways but in cooperation with one another.

Historical Context

The famous victory of Lapu-Lapu against Ferdinand Magellan is one of the earliest examples of resistance in the archipelago. It has high symbolic value. A considerable number of Lapu-Lapu's men defeated the well-armed and battle-hardened Spanish conquistadores in a low-tide clash along the shores of Mactan in 1521. One narrative speaks of a rivalry between Lapu-Lapu and Rajah Humabon, a rivalry that Magellan used by teaming up with the latter in order to attack the former. Another emphasizes that Lapu-Lapu's group was set to defend the autonomy of their community.

Prior to the nationalist struggle, the so-called Moro Wars lasted from 1565 to 1898,[3] preventing the Spaniards from subjugating the inhabitants of the southern part of the archipelago. Colonizers mobilized Christianized locals to fight Muslims, thus laying the foundation of the "perpetual" Christian-Muslim conflict in Mindanao.

The Philippines was one of the first Asian countries to stage a revolution against the colonialism of the West. The early phase of the Filipino struggle was carried by local privileged

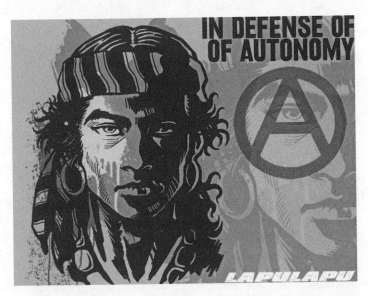

intellectuals like José Rizal and Marcelo del Pilar. The revolution was nationalist in character, which is understandable, as, at the time, nationalism was propagated in many parts of the world, especially Europe. This profoundly influenced Rizal's work and inspired the oppressed masses, culminating in armed resistance organized by Andrés Bonifacio in 1896.

With the growing influence of the US, combined with the simultaneous armed resistance in Cuba, the Filipino nationalist resistance was able to substantially reduce the influence of the Catholics and finally drive them out of colonial Spain. But American expansionist policies immediately took effect, as expressed through the 1898 Treaty of Paris.[4] Shortly after the inauguration of the First Philippine Republic in January 1899, the Filipino-American War broke out, claiming six hundred thousand Filipino lives, mostly due to starvation and disease.

The revolutionary tradition in the country was enriched by the arrival of Isabelo de los Reyes in Manila in 1901 from his exile in Barcelona, Spain. He brought a collection of books with him, including some by Errico Malatesta, Pierre-Joseph Proudhon, Peter Kropotkin, Karl Marx, Charles Darwin,

Thomas Aquinas, and Voltaire. This was followed by a successful wave of protests and strikes within and around Manila that paved the way for the establishment of the Unión Obrera Democrática (UOD). This marked the shift of the revolutionary struggle from a mere nationalist to an anti-imperialist one.

The UOD disintegrated in 1903. From its remains, the Socialist Party was established, which later led the Hukbalahap guerilla movement, active from 1942 to 1954. Its members were the foremost opponents of the Japanese forces prior to the reinforcement provided by the Americans. This was also the period when the revolutionary movement was increasingly influenced by Bolshevik ideas.

In the late 1960s, the Maoist-influenced Communist Party was established. It adopted a nationalist strategy and protracted the people's war. It gained enormous support from the masses but failed to grab power. In 1992, a split led to a fragmentation into smaller party formations.

Hard Facts in the Current Context

Indeed, the country's historical development has continuously enriched its revolutionary tradition, not to mention the resistance efforts outside of the national democracy movement, such as sectoral and community-based resistance and the Moro struggle, among others.

However, such richness failed to translate immediately into the interest of the people. In the 1970s, the poverty rate was as high as 40 percent. The current rate is 34 to 36 percent according to the National Statistical Coordination Board.[5] This indicates only marginal improvement in terms of poverty reduction.

Unemployment, on the other hand, is stagnant at eleven million, while underemployment is up to seven million. This is aggravated by the massive destruction of our natural resources due to the growth orientation of the economy and the incapacity of the state to manage and utilize them in a sustainable way.

Furthermore, liberalization, coupled with chronic rent-seeking practices in government offices and the absence of a logical economic development plan, inflicted serious injury to the domestic economy, which further exacerbated our deteriorating economic condition.

Another equally important issue is the marginalization of huge numbers of citizens in decision-making processes that directly and indirectly affect their political, social, and economic lives. The existing political structure makes citizens passive, inactive, and apathetic. Their political participation is reduced to routine electoral exercises where they will occasionally choose politicians who will represent them in making and implementing policies.

We can hardly identify a historical period when Filipinos lived in prosperity, abundance, and relative peace, except during pre-Spanish times. As described by Italian explorer Antonio Pigafetta, the inhabitants of the archipelago were in perfect health and had no physical defects. He got the impression that food scarcity was not prevalent.[6] While William Henry Scott and a host of other writers confirmed the presence of slavery in the archipelago during the pre-Spanish period, they never mentioned any sign of poverty in local villages.[7]

These findings make us think that the phenomenon of poverty in the Philippines occurred with the advent of Spanish colonization and coercive formation of a centralized government. Unfortunately, several studies have conveniently pinned down population explosion as the cause of poverty, thus undermining the fact that it was brought about by systemic oppression. For instance, in Southern Asia, around thirty million households own no or very little land, representing 40 percent of nearly all rural households on the subcontinent. Both the African and Latin American continents have similar data. Moreover, land distribution in the nations of the South favors large-scale commercial agriculture controlled by a few landowners. Ergo, poverty is rooted socially.

In 2000, the Philippines ranked seventy-seventh out of more than 150 countries, with a poverty level of 34 percent and a Human Development Index (HDI) of 0.656.[8] According to the 1993 Fishery Sector Program Report of the Asian Development Bank, 80 percent of fisher households lived below the poverty line. Four primary factors are widely accepted by those studying the fishery sector:

1) low productivity of land-based resources or lack of access to land;
2) low productivity of aquatic resources due mainly to habitat destruction and stock depletion;
3) resource use conflict, particularly in coastal waters;
4) lack of adequate basic services, i.e., health, education, shelter, and infrastructure.

The report also cited high population density in most near-shore areas. We know for a fact that the increase of population in coastal communities is due to migration. As noted in an ASEAN-SEAFDEC (Association of Southeast Asian Nations-Southeast Asian Fisheries Development Center) report in 2001, households displaced in agricultural lands seek economic opportunity in coastal areas that are open to anybody who wants to use fishery resources. Poverty is, therefore, not rooted in natural limits; it is clearly brought on by structural problems, such as the distribution of wealth and the control of natural resources.

The idea of a carrying capacity is well-recognized. It refers to a limit for both the number of organisms and the non-living matter in specific ecosystems, based on the availability of food, space, and other vital things for their existence. A specific ecosystem is able to absorb pressure brought on by extraction. But the destruction of natural resources (which results in the death of many citizens and the loss of livelihoods) is not directly attributable to population numbers. In fact, it is common knowledge that big corporations benefit from large-scale logging operations. Together with large commercial mining operations, this eventually leads to the denudation of our forests. It must also be noted that mineral extraction is one of the notorious polluters of the coastal zones and significantly reduces fish stocks.

There is not sufficient evidence to prove that the country's population of eighty-six million challenges the carrying capacity of the local ecosystems. Clearly, food production is no longer a problem. In fact, developed nations—as well as developing nations like China, India, and Brazil—are extra-aggressive in bilateral and multilateral trade agreements, in order to have full market access to the economies of poor and other nations where they can dump their huge surpluses. The available data on poverty in the Philippines is related to low agricultural and fishery productivity and poor economic performance; this, in turn, can be directly traced to government negligence, incompetence, irresponsibility, and nonaccountability. Poverty is caused by unemployment, lack of land to till, degradation of natural resources, lack of economic opportunity, lack of social services, corruption, and the absence of a logical economic development agenda.

The huge profits being produced through massive extraction of natural resources do not deliver anything concrete to the people. We have enough sources of food to feed the entire population due to the highly abundant natural resources of the archipelago. But the use of our resources only fuels economic growth or sustains the greed for profit of the elite.

With this in mind, we should know that in order to establish a society that is free, equitable, and rational, capitalism must be abolished and oppressive hierarchical political systems must be replaced by a system where citizens are highly involved in all political exercises, specifically in decision-making.

The Logic of Centralizing Power

In the sixteenth century, the state was described as a large-scale governmental organization effectively centralized by means of strictly secular bureaucracy, often implemented by some kind of representative body. Since economic activities profoundly influence the operations of centralized govern- ments, the state's definition continuously evolved, but its orig- inal nature—that is, to concentrate power and its desire to increase inexorable sovereignty—did not and will not change. Another important consideration is that the state is the only institution that can use legitimate violence against those who do not recognize its hegemony. Theoretically, political power resides only in the state, but complete concentration of power is impossible. The existence of the state depends on *relatively* concentrated power.

The hierarchical nature of the state inevitably creates a bureaucracy that concentrates governance and decision- making in a few representatives, akin to the institutional arrangement of the red bureaucracy, corporate structures, and the churches' organigram. But a handful of representa- tives do not constitute a democracy; on the contrary, they constitute nothing but the rule of a few. Democracy will only be realized through meaningful and substantial participation of the people in a politics they can understand, appreciate, relate and contribute to, perform in, benefit from, and in which they share duties and responsibilities.

The question is: How are we going to involve ordinary people in political exercises if they do not have any interest in engaging in politics? Their disinterest might be rooted in the fact that the current political system does not offer anything to the people. All is reduced to promises and rhetoric. For the common people, politics requires complicated technical skills and knowledge that can only be earned in prestigious and expensive universities. It also seems to require both a technical jargon and expensive outfits, which solidifies the impression that politics is an enterprise solely for the rich and educated. The term *polis*, as we trace it back to the tradition of the Greeks, refers to the management of the community by the citizens. This meaning has apparently been lost due to a statism, which has turned politics into a lucrative career option that marginalizes ordinary people.

Our effort in imagining alternatives beyond the politics of the state will be facilitated by regaining the lost meaning of "politics" and calibrating it in our own context.

Libertarian Alternatives

Anarchist alternatives, as reflected by the October 1917 Revolution, were characterized by spontaneity and the self-organized revolt of the masses. Powerful united fronts of various forces developed and crushed the oppressive Czarist regime within three days. The massive unrest of the people and other heterogeneous elements led to the abolition of the old regime without any specific alternative model and without instruction from any group. The majority of the masses did not directly articulate the ideas espoused by the anarcho-syndicalists, but what the people had done was exactly what the anarcho-syndicalists had in mind. Upon the abolition of the Czarist state, the people spontaneously organized themselves. In Kronstadt, houses were socialized through the house committees which extended to entire streets and resulted in the creation of street and block committees. The same thing happened in Petrograd. The factory committees that appeared almost out of nowhere were geared toward establishing "producer-consumer communes."

During the Spanish Civil War, the eastern part of Spain was under strong influence of the anarchist movement. There was direct workers' management in industrial and commercial establishments through the 2,000 collectives in Catalonia. In February 1937, 275 peasant and farm workers' collectives with a total of 80,000 members were formed in Aragon near the front line. They occupied vast lands which had been abandoned by their landlords. In three months, these collectives increased to 450, with a total number of 180,000 members.

There are a lot of experiences worth citing from Latin America, Asia, and Africa, but these are poorly studied and seldom mentioned in our history books. The anarchist movement is barely mentioned, despite its profound influence in the early stages of Philippine nationalist resistance and the anti-imperialist struggle in the archipelago.

Direct Democracy

Direct democracy is not a new idea. It was and is still being practiced in many parts of the world. But the concept is poorly explored due to the power-hungry behavior of the political and economic elites, as well as leftists who advocate and practice authoritarianism.

To refresh our minds, the original Greek meaning of politics comes from the word *polis*, which entails that the citizens directly formulate public policies through face-to-face processes called assemblies, which are based on the ethics of complementarity and solidarity. Of course, the implementation of the idea was flawed due the fact that only those who owned slaves and had the luxury of time to participate in community management counted as citizens. But the idea of direct democracy proved nonetheless workable.

Confederal structures have appeared in history time and time again, like those of the sixteenth-century Spanish *communeros* or the American town meetings of the 1770s. Other examples include the Parisian revolutionary sections of the 1790s, the Paris Commune of 1871, and so on.

Instead of organizing a political party, why do we not go back to such assemblies? Political parties claim that they have an organized network and mass base. In some cases, they do; we will not try to refute this. We are concerned with the kind of politics that they employ. Their organizational setup is inherently top-down due to a representational system in which a few individuals from the party represent the interests of the entire nation. This breeds bossism, where a few people form the apex of the hierarchy. Moreover, these people have authority vis-à-vis their members, which will eventually end in a "leader and led" relationship. People become simple pawns. Instead of having active, creative, imaginative, and dynamic citizens, we have passive and mechanized constituents whose duty is reduced to the occasional attendance of mass meetings and a routine selection of leaders that merely reinforces the culture of obedience.

Democracy is not about creating obedient followers. It is not about imposing uniform rules on a complex and diverse population with regard to people's interests, views, ways of life, prejudices, economic activities, the social and natural environment, culture, and spiritual life. Rather, democracy is about creating a political atmosphere which is participatory and inclusive of a highly diverse population, and which is based on the actual needs and interests of the communities.

We do not intend to undermine the initiative certain political parties take when it comes to advancing the interests of the communities. Yet, since leftist movements are in the minority, maybe it would make sense for them to strive more to gain political value and leverage in order to mobilize the people instead of engaging in party politics. As parties, their interests are not necessarily identical with those of the communities, since the latter are characterized by a diversity the parties seldom represent. Traditionally, leftist parties are class-based and have a great tendency to overlook other sectors and groups who are also exploited and are often significant in number. This approach often fosters elitism in the glorified class.

In a broad sense, direct democracy will be applied by organizing free assemblies at the local level. People's organizations that are based on communal interests, including those of peasants, fishers, women, youth, indigenous people, vendors, tricycle drivers, jeepney drivers, the homeless, gays, neighborhood associations, religious groups, and other formations at the local level, should be encouraged to organize themselves.

Based on experience, people will surely participate in political processes if the topic to be discussed is directly related to their interests, their daily activities, and the immediate and strategic needs of their communities. People will conduct face-to-face meetings at the *barangay* (village) level to tackle their immediate concerns; they will share ideas, duties, and responsibilities to address their issues in relation to other barangays. They are encouraged to engage in discussions and debates on public facilities using their own language and the existing local mechanisms to facilitate local political mechanisms.

Obviously, an ideal political structure should not mobilize people for the purpose of elevating the political value of certain political parties for elections or for the goal of taking political power, which will merely reinforce the inactivity of their constituents. The political structure we envision will bring the political arena to the very doorstep of the people; it will create a political atmosphere that encourages the citizens' active, creative, imaginative, and dynamic participation. The ultimate direction of this process is to empower the vast number of marginalized citizens from below. This politics is educative, since it will enhance the people's capacity to democratically discuss, decide, formulate, and implement plans with regard to their common resources and their own affairs.

Confederation

In general, the pre-Spanish barangays were interdependent but loosely federated. Among their bases of interaction were trade, commerce, and war (raids for slaves and wives and for revenge). Highly federated barangays were usually found in river mouths or wherever the ports were strategically located for commerce and where economic activities were high. This is not to romanticize the idea of the baranganic system but, rather, to trace our traditional practice of decentralism, which actually proved to be far more humane than the statist model that was imposed by the colonialists and that is still in place today.

Our idea of decentralization here should not be mistaken as parochialism, which might lead to the isolation of a locality from the rest of world. Confederalism, as defined by Murray Bookchin, is "above all a network of administrative councils whose members or delegates are elected from popular, face-to-face democratic assemblies."[9] In our context, structures will be independently organized at a barangay or community level. Every barangay or community assembly will elect delegates whose function is purely administrative, such as transmitting information and taking care of other practicalities. Policy-making will take place strictly at the popular assemblies in the barangay and on the community level. Delegates have no power to decide, and they are totally recallable and accountable to the assemblies that mandate them. More importantly, delegates possess no privilege and authority over the citizens.

Confederal councils comprised of substantial delegates will be organized at the municipal level. Then municipalities will be confederated at the provincial level. The provincial level will then comprise the Archipelagic Confederation.

A confederation is a structure that connects and interlinks politically and economically every community that belongs to it, and whose functions are administrative and coordinative. The ultimate idea of a confederation is to integrate all social structures—not in a hierarchical or top-down manner but, rather, the opposite. Public policies will be formulated from the grassroots, which will be expressed at the municipal and provincial levels. The basis of integration is not competition but mutual cooperation, complementation, and solidarity. Every sector, group, and other formation of the municipality will find its place in production processes to ensure the needs of the communities.

We cannot blame groups used to the party system and the statist model if they instinctively express a low appreciation for the proposed alternative view. Indeed, taking political power is a shortcut to institute desired changes, but such changes are not necessarily meaningful for those who did not participate in the seizure of political power. In many instances, the masses remain reduced to the status of mere spectators to the political exercise initiated by the few. Once again, they are made passive, inactive, and obedient constituents.

Our process is strategic, because it also involves changing the behavior of people who are highly influenced by the dominant institutions that promote and reinforce an order based on competition, individualism, and imposed uniformity. As part of the processes that resist the current order and the behavior that reinforces it, direct democracy can be employed. In the heist of the brutal effect of grow-or-die market capitalism and a corrupt centralized state, communities should persistently defend their own physical and social space by defining its specific interests in connection to larger communities. We should encourage locals to self-organize and maximize their traditional networks to protect and advance the interests of their localities in relation to the interests and needs of other communities.

NOTES
All notes in this essay by the editor.
1   The Expanded Value Added Tax (E-VAT) is a form of sales tax that is imposed on the sale of goods and services and on the import of goods into the Philippines.
2   The Communist Party of the Philippines (CCP) was founded in 1968. The New People's Army (NPA) is its armed wing. The National Democratic Front (NDF), founded in 1973, is a radical left umbrella organization that includes the CCP and NPA.
3   The Moro people inhabit the southernmost islands of the Philippines. They are predominantly of Muslim faith.
4   The Treaty of Paris of 1898 ended the Spanish-American War and transferred the colonial possession of Cuba, Puerto Rico, Guam, and the Philippines to the United States.
5   The National Statistical Coordination Board was established in 1987. In 2013, it merged with other government agencies into the Philippine Statistics Authority.
6   Antonio Pigafetta (c. 1491–c. 1531), a member of the 1519–1522 expedition to the Philippines led by Ferninand Magellan, left a detailed journal of the journey.
7   See William Henry Scott, *Barangay: Sixteenth-Century Philippine Culture and Society* (Manila: Ateneo de Manila University Press, 1997).

8 It is unclear where these figures were derived from. The UN's *Human Development Report 2000* lists the Philippines' HDI at 0.744 and the poverty rate at 37.5 percent.

9 Murray Bookchin, *Urbanization without Cities: The Rise and Decline of Citizenship* (Montreal: Black Rose Books, 1992), 297.

A PATHOLOGY IN OUR FILIPINO IDENTITY
A Disease That Decayed the Archipelago's Freedom and Prosperity
(2011)

Despite many discussions about the exact definition, myriad countries around the world adopted the idea of a *nation*. In his book *Imagined Communities*, Benedict Anderson quoted quite a good number of authors who failed to provide a proper definition. Anderson concludes that the notion can only be understood through historical analysis.

Let us take a quick glance at some significant parts of our own history to understand the development of the archipelago into a nation.

The Exogenous Factor: The Evil Empire from the West
The menace of expansionist policies from the West changed the lives of our ancestors forever. The consequences of these changes still determine our lives today: poverty, ignorance, subjugation, political marginalization, loss of identity and self-determination, resource degradation.

Ferdinand Magellan kept his word to King Charles I of Spain, passed the great American continent, and indeed opened a new route to the Spice Islands. The galleon *Trinidad* reached first Limasawa, then Cebu.

Lapu-Lapu's uncompromising attitude against the Spaniards proved to be right, and Rajah Humabon's hostile behavior toward them later might indicate his realization about the diabolic intentions of these newcomers.

The Spanish government sent more expeditions between 1525 and 1542. The one of Miguel López de Legaspi was the breakthrough. Upon receiving orders from the Audencia of Mexico, four ships carrying 350 men sailed off to the archipelago and successfully captured Cebu, and later Manila and its surrounding provinces.

From then on, the regalian doctrine took hold in the archipelago based on the capacity of the centralized government that received orders from Spain. This meant that all natural resources of the archipelago became royal property and all of its inhabitants royal subjects with obligations to obey royal orders.

The Internal Weakness: Spirits Subdued

The Spaniards imposed a new social order, wherein political, economic, and cultural affairs were centralized under their control. An abstract large-scale community—an organized, centralized structure—was introduced, but not without blood. Pockets of resistance emerged—led by Tamblot on Bohol, Bancao on Leyte, Sumuroy on Samar, and Tapar in the province of Iloilo. Those led by Dabao in northern Mindanao, Pedro Gumapos and, later, Diego and Gabriela Silang in Vigan, as well as the Basi Revolt in Ilocos Norte scored substantial successes but were quickly subdued.

Oppressive policies and practices, such as *encomienda*,[1] taxation, the polo system, and discrimination, caused revolts. Christianity, however, was successful. Successive missionaries captured our ancestors' deep spirituality, thus winning their loyalty, which explained numerous cases of betrayal that caused revolts to fail. Had our ancestors discovered that they could use traditional archipelagic networks of support, they could have won.

It is difficult to know when the people in the archipelago began to consider themselves a nation rather than simply Tagalogs, Ilokanos, Visayans, or members of a specific tribe. However, it is reasonable to suppose that the oppressive conditions established common sentiments against the colonizers.

Diseases from the West, or Baranganic Resistance Abandoned

The oppressive conditions that could not be transcended by the pockets of resistance continued until the Enlightenment. Reason and science prevailed and became influential on the global scale. Rebels and intellectuals like Andrés Bonifacio, José Rizal, Marcelo del Pilar, Graciano López Jaena,[2] and others used this influence from European ideas to drive the Spaniards away.

The revolutionary nationalist organization Katipunan, founded in 1892, claimed sovereignty. Sovereignty would mean the abolition of oppressive conditions that were approved by huge numbers of the poor and underprivileged. This was to be done by staging revolution and creating a republic with a centralized government that would rule the entire archipelago. The community beyond face-to-face politics was to be reinforced further.

The few privileged had their own way of creating nationhood. According to Josephine Dionisio's introduction to Randy David's book *Nation, Self and Citizenship: An Invitation to Philippine Sociology* (2002), the Filipino nation is in part an invention of European-educated Filipino intellectuals who we know now as our heroes.

Katipunan and its idea of sovereignty became the viable expression of freedom to many locals who were already influenced by the centralistic system brought by the Spanish monarchy and its political organizations.

The primitive autonomous and interdependent *barangays* were not sufficient to resist the organizational patterns of the colonizers said to be superior to the primitive structures. But this was only true if we measure superiority by conquest. The colonial patterns are designed to colonize, while the primitive structures are characterized by cooperation, diversity, and the absence of private property.

The context discussed above reinforced the idea of statism among the rebels. The conceived territory which is the archipelago was to be governed by a uniform centralized political power that later expounded a statist Pan-Germanic form of nationalism.

The term *Tagalog*, used by Bonifacio, refers to the entire archipelago. It represents our early concept of a nation. The concepts of *inang bayan* (motherland) and *haring bayan* (sovereign nation) are the earliest representations of the idea of nationhood (imagined large-scale communities) among the Katipuneros and their supporters. "Imagined," because the face-to-face process of barangays was replaced by highly centralized political organizations based on the idea of republicanism and representative democracy, generally derived from the principles of *The Declaration of the Rights of Man and of the Citizen* of the 1789 revolutionary National Assembly of France.

Filipino Identity, a Product of Coercive Processes

As history shows, the idea of the Philippines as a nation is due to long coercive processes of colonization that continue to this day. Physically, the colonizers are gone, but their supremacy deeply and profoundly penetrates our values and prejudices, our culture and our developmental perspective.

Anderson considered nationalism a pathology in our modern developmental history. The Philippines as a nation is indeed a pathology that decayed our autonomous traditions and interdependent relations of mutual cooperation.

Nationalism and statism are illnesses that destroyed the desirable conditions of the primitive communities in the archipelago. Primitive barangays did engage in warfare among themselves. For instance, inhabitants of Mindanao and Panay exchanged attacks on a regular basis. Tribal war, commonly known as head-hunting, was also typical among tribes in northern Luzon. Largely, common causes of attacks and raids were revenge, betrayal of a pact, and unresolved disputes of territorial claims, but not to dominate and to rule.

Highly decentralized these communities were, but in permanent warfare they were not. Interdependent relations provided overall mutual protection and benefits and were common among primitive communities.

The term *Filipino* originally referred to an individual born in the archipelago by Spanish parents. Currently, many of us regard "Filipino" as our superior identity that is upheld by many subgroups and tribes, being dependent on ethnolinguistic identity and geographical affiliation in the archipelago. This goes for basically everyone except tribes that remain isolated and people in the southern Philippines who aim to secede and to establish a Muslim nation.

Our sense of nationalism and identity as "Filipino" was particularly high during the times when revolutionary fervor was strong within us, especially during the Katipunan uprising and the People Power Revolution of 1986. However, the meaning of our identity as "Filipino" continuously changes. After the two major political exercises of EDSA,[3] social and economic conditions have not changed. Unemployment is steadily increasing, hunger is prevalent, political marginalization is alarming, and ecological destruction is rampant throughout the archipelago and has caused the loss of the livelihoods of millions. While billions of pesos were already spent on agrarian reform during the Aquino regime, this reform is still far from completion.

Prices of basic commodities are increasing fast, while workers' wages barely move. The peso is gaining strength in relation to the dollar to the detriment of the Overseas Filipino Workers (OFWs), who deliver substantial value in government revenues. Corruption is deemed acceptable in our culture.

We are maids in Europe and Singapore, prostitutes in Japan, and underpaid workers in the international seafaring industry, while the characteristics of our lives at home are obedience, passivity, individualism, opportunism, corruption, and dependency, due to exogenous forces brought on by colonization, the centralization of power, capitalism, and social relations based on competition and hierarchy. These conditions further facilitate the process of decadence of the meaning of "Filipino" that was established through coercive processes.

Upon acquiring ideas from the West, native rebels felt compelled to adopt and invent "Filipino" as a national identity to effectively fight Spanish colonizers. The statist framework that governed the Katipunan reinforced this, and we totally veered away from the decentralized ways of the primitive barangays.

Ultimately, the creation of our identity as a nation and as "Filipino" did not come from our own cultural, political, and social conditions and self-determination. It came from oppression, slavery, aggression, and the dominance of the West. The pioneer dwellers of the archipelago up to the baranganic phase were not Christians or republicans or parliamentarians or corporate leaders or bureaucrats. They were hunters, gatherers, fishers, and farmers with their own industries. They had their own decentralized system of politics, autonomous and interdependent. They had a rich culture and a generally prosperous economy that sustained massive trading activities with China, Malaysia, Indonesia, and even Siam (Thailand).

José Rizal wrote in his essay *The Indolence of the Filipino*:

> All the histories of those first years, in short, abound
> in long accounts about the industry and agriculture
> of the natives: mines, gold-washings, looms, farms,
> barter, naval construction, raising of poultry and stock,
> weaving of silk and cotton, distilleries, manufactures
> of arms, pearl fisheries, the civet industry, the horn
> and hide industry, etc., are things encountered at every
> step, and, considering the time and the conditions in
> the islands, prove that there was life, there was activity,
> there was movement.[4]

He further explained:

And not only Morga, not only Chirino, Colin, Argensola, Gaspar de San Agustin and others agree in this matter, but modern travelers, after two hundred and fifty years, examining the decadence and misery, assert the same thing. Dr. Hans Meyer, when he saw the unsubdued tribes cultivating beautiful fields and working energetically, asked if they would not become indolent when they in turn should accept Christianity and a paternal government.[5]

Evidently, the state—through its government and with the help of Christianity—oppressed, enslaved, and corrupted our souls, while at the same time creating and reinforcing the Filipino identity and nation.

The Philippine nation and the Filipino citizen have never delivered concrete expressions of democracy and prosperity for the lives of the many. In fact, these notions undermined the freedom and abundance of the primitive communities.

I do not propose splitting up into several unrelated and hostile groups or anything like that. The earlier discussion informed us already that this is not part of the autonomous and interdependent wisdom that I wish to explore. The theme of mutual cooperation and the absence of social stratification characterized the primitive communities, particularly Pisan tribal groups, from about 50,000 to 500 BCE. We can gain insight from this in order to imagine our future political communities; communities that will allow total diversity and that will concretely address social problems like poverty, ignorance, massive ecological destruction, as well as all forms of abuse, discrimination, and political marginalization.

Reestablishing this decentralized system within a non-statist framework is a sound proposition, particularly because the statist alternatives are increasingly losing their appeal to the inhabitants of the archipelago. Redefining "Filipino" based on a non-statist paradigm is key to overcoming the mentioned social problems. Reviving our lost identity means regaining our lost freedom and abundance from the centralistic systems of the state and capitalism.

In our modern age, decentralized, autonomous, and interdependent could mean the following: direct workers' control of industries and factories; direct management of employees of the former government institutions for administrative functions; the collectivization of agricultural lands; direct community management of ecosystems; total respect and recognition of the indigenous claims to ancestral lands and waters; direct participation of the community, producers, workers, women, youth, gays, lesbians, senior citizens, and sidewalk vendors in economic and social planning; the socialization of facilities like housing, health services, water, and energy supply—substantial time for socialization is an essential human activity that must be reinstituted in the actual application of direct democracy.

Making politics accessible to every Filipino family is what counts. What we need is the widest participation of the people from the communities and localities. The system of representative democracy is not designed to accommodate people's participation in power, and we must replace this with direct democracy, a political system that offers a true participation in power by being organized in a decentralized fashion based on the principles of solidarity and mutual cooperation.

The proposed system requires a dialectical process of educating citizens in every municipality and barangay with regard to the idea of self-determination, deep and radical ecological awareness, cooperation, solidarity, mutuality, diversity, and productivity. In a broad stroke, these processes will bring people to voluntarily organize at the municipal, city, or barangay level based on their interests. Voluntary structures will actively participate in decision-making at public places facilitated by administrative councils. It should be noted that members of administrative councils function only to facilitate the implementation of the agreed system. They do not have any authority or privilege.

Idealism is our only hope. The survival of humanity is connected to the health of the global ecology. Its condition is deteriorating fast. This is due to anthropocentrism and hierarchical relations among human beings.

The higher the position in a hierarchical structure the greater the access to power and benefits. This promotes competition and relations between people that revolve around incentives and privilege. Incentives entice people to produce more for markets and shops, which will result in massive extraction of natural resources and the treatment of the earth as a sink. This causes ecological crises. Accumulation of incentives of the few winners leads to poverty and the marginalization of the many.

Before the global ecology turns into total waste, the people of the world must find ways to innovate social relations and systems that will replace political hierarchies and the centralization of incentives and benefit streams. We must do it swiftly.

NOTES
All notes in this article by the editor.

1   An *encomienda* bestowed upon Spanish colonists in Latin America the right to demand tribute and forced labor from the indigenous people.

2   Graciano López Jaena (1856–1896) was a journalist in Spanish exile and a leading figure in the Propaganda Movement.

3   See page 23, note 8.

4   José Rizal, *The Indolence of the Filipino*, quoted from www.fullbooks. com/The-Indolence-of-the-Filipino.html. The essay originally appeared in 1890 in Spanish in the newspaper *La Solidaridad*, an important organ of the Propaganda Movement.

5   Ibid.

RECONNECTING TRADITIONAL LINKS
A Contribution to Understanding the Sabah Crisis (2013)

Background: the Sabah crisis, also known as the "Lahad Datu standoff," occurred in March–April 2013, when 235 militants claiming to belong to the "Royal Security Forces of the Sultanate of Sulu and North Borneo" occupied an area in the Lahad Datu district of the Malaysian state of Sabah. They had arrived by boat from the island of Simunul in the southern Philippines, sent by Jamalul Kiram III (1938–2013), who claimed to rule over the Sultanate of Sulu, which has not been officially recognized since 1986. After a six-week standoff, Malaysian security forces regained control of the area, killing sixty-five of the occupiers.
—the editor

The Tausūg by tradition are warriors. They have a history of resisting invasion with violent confrontation. They are known for being tenacious and would not easily back down in asserting their autonomy. Way back, during Spanish and American colonization, the Tausūg were among the fiercest enemies of the imperialists. During the Philippine-American War, the Americans invented the .45 caliber handgun and made it standard for its cavalry due to the .38 caliber handgun not being able to stop the oncoming Tausūg warriors, who were wrapped in cloth to prevent hemorrhage caused by bullets. Currently, Tausūg warriors are also involved in the armed struggle for autonomy in the southern part of the Philippines.

With this background, one could easily assume that the Tausūg came to occupy Sabah in order to settle the Sabah conflict by claiming parts of the island through armed confrontation. It could be assumed that through their long experience of combat they acquired the ability to prevent casualties on their part. Their experience in war instructs them not to attack the enemy where it has great military advantage and not to provoke an enemy powerful enough to crush them.

Based on public statements by Sultan Kiram III, however, they came to Sabah peacefully to claim the area as a part of their ancestral domain. They went there to establish their physical presence through nonviolent means and to join the thousands of so-called Filipinos already staying there. They did not attack and only prepared to defend themselves against hostile elements. Aside from historical links, the Kirams also possessed documents that reinforced their claims.

The Malaysian government intentionally sent a wrong signal to the public when it announced that the Tausūg "invaded" Sabah. It was a threatening statement to legitimize their military operations against the Tausūg and against the poor people of Lahad Datu and the surrounding communities. Worse, the Malaysian government issued a statement branding the Tausūg as terrorists, which provided the justification to slaughter them.

The Malaysian government overreacted and deployed tanks, helicopters, and even submarines. Since the crises has broken out, sixty-three deaths and ninety-seven arrests related to the occupation have been reported.

Just like the with the Spratly Islands,[1] it is widely believed that Sabah has oil deposits. The Malaysian government is surely aware of this, so it is plausible to think that it is not the "invasion" that worries them most.

On behalf of the Filipino people, Benigno Aquino III, the current president, issued an order contradicting the interests of the indigenous Tausūg's claim by ordering them to back down. He should be reminded that before the Spaniards came,

the communities of the archipelago were part of a macrosoci-
ety tied together by kinship and trade—not only in Mindanao
but also in the Visayas and on Luzon. The Philippine archipelago was tightly linked to Malacca, Indonesia, Malaysia,
Thailand, and other communities in Southeast Asia. As the
imperialists divided the Southeast Asian region, they disconnected these links and a network that had been established
throughout a long indigenous process.

The current crisis is therefore a manifestation of a deeply
rooted complexity that cannot be resolved by enforcing a
nationalist framework and by coercing people into recognizing
systems that are alien to the communities of the archipelago.

Traditionally, we were not bound by the limits of nation-
states; the lifestyles of our ancestors were as fluid as the tide
of the oceans that connect us. In fact, the families of Lakan
Dula, Rajah Matanda, and Rajah Sulayman that formerly
occupied Manila, Tondo, Bulacan, Sulu, and Borneo were
linked by affinity and consanguinity.[2]

Sultan Kiram III and his followers have already been
found guilty; the Malaysian government does not heed calls
for a ceasefire and conducts more military raids instead. The
Philippine government's only effort is to offer a mercy ship,
which is an insult to the direct action and courageous deeds
of the Tausūg.

We do not agree with waging war, and we condemn those
who cause hostilities; we condemn the Malaysian government
for its decision to launch an all-out offensive despite calls for
a ceasefire.

We also condemn the Philippine government because
of its incapacity to handle the conflict. Its insensitivity and
insincerity became clear when Benigno Aquino III asked the
Tausūg to go home. Instead of preparing a lawsuit against
Kiram, a dialogue could have been arranged to hear the
Tausūg's side. The government could have offered assurances
it would explore all possible venues like the United Nations.
That way, the betrayal of the Tausūg could have been avoided.

We understand the sensitivity of the issue, and we fear an escalation and an even bigger military confrontation. Careful negotiation is needed. The political advisers of PNoy, as Benigno Aquino III is known by many, are perhaps convinced of the inferiority of the Philippine military. But no one is talking about a war. The Philippine government has plenty of peaceful options in dealing with the Malaysian government without putting the Tausūg in an undignified situation.

Seeking a long-lasting solution to this conflict is beneficial to many of us, as the thick layers of animosity and hatred caused by hundreds of years of coercion and exploitation have already claimed thousands of lives. Respect for self-determination and the recognition of the tradition of self-organizing are meaningful ways to start finding peace and development.

The organizational arrangement of the Tausūg in a sultanate is surely not perfect; it is characterized by social stratification and an unequal distribution of wealth. Leaders enjoy the same privileges as corporate leaders and other beneficiaries of hierarchical institutions. Changing these hierarchical systems is always a focus of our work and the desire of many communities aspiring to attain freedom and prosperity. But asserting rights over indigenous space and autonomy is a radical step against the hegemony of the nation-state. This is the most important aspect of the occupation of Sabah.

NOTES

All notes in this article by the editor.

1   The contested Spratly Islands in the South China Sea are claimed by various countries: China, Taiwan, Brunei, Malaysia, Vietnam, and the Philippines.

2   Lakan Dula (c. 1503–1575), Rajah Matanda (1480–1572), and Rajah Sulayman (1558–1575) were precolonial political leaders in the archipelago that was to become known as the Philippines.

DIALECTICAL HISTORICAL MATERIALISM

An Effective Tool for Authoritarian Politics, Dominance, and Control in the Archipelago (2017)

For many years, Marxism has been the dominant ideology among dissenters in the archipelago. It is a convenient tool utilized by social movements, civil society, scholars, academics, and even a few government agents. The Marxist framework deeply influenced the way we view our history and social alternatives. Its evolutionary logic provides analysis and proposes sets of actions.

Historical accounts showed that resistance is not new to indigenous communities in the archipelago. Our ancestors were not dumb; indigenous people do not need to borrow ideas from the West to realize their own situation. Indigenous communities have mechanisms designed to protect and sustain their existence, culture, and well-being.

Resistance that led to violent confrontation and war in different regions of the archipelago was complex. Every resistance has a peculiarity based on its context, culture, and time. But statist politics became the dominant framework among those who have challenged the status quo, because dominance is the very nature of the state. This kind of politics greatly affected the conduct of local dissent which led to the establishment of republican and leftist institutions.

Marxism in the archipelago that we today call the "Philippines" has many variations. Like the dominant religions, Marxism produced a variety of thinkers, ideologues,

politicians, activists, and even faith-based groups and individuals.

Dialectical historical materialism (DHM) is one of Marxism's fundamentals to analyze society. It has been widely criticized for putting too much emphasis on the economy. It reduces social complexities through a focus on economic progress and relates the benchmark of development to the scale of production and accumulation of material wealth. It disregards other essential aspects of society by elevating one class to the pedestal of the revolution.

It has been said that capitalism will prepare the material and social capital for the establishment of a socialist society. Since workers are the primary force of production in a capitalist society, Marxists believe that the proletariat will lead the revolution with the aim to establish a "dictatorship."

Social revolution is a process of overhauling social relationships that reinforce inequality, social injustice,

environmental destruction, and patriarchy. This process can only be realized if heterogeneous agents of society participate. The workers' role is to liberate themselves from the chains of capitalism; women should act against patriarchy; other sectors and classes must do their share for social change by acting directly in their interests. Social revolution will not take place if the people's mode of thinking is generally respectful to the institutions that reproduce and reinforce rules that define property, ownership, privileges, norms, and power. Putting a particular class or group on a pedestal is another form of hierarchy and invites privilege and the centralization of power.

In relation to this criticism, I would like to reiterate that the dialectical process is hierarchical. It is no different from the "band-tribe-chiefdom-state" model pioneered by the archeologist Elman Service, which refers to the hierarchical progression of society and presents an evolutionary process of community from simple stateless egalitarian indigenous organizations like bands and tribes to chiefdoms and states, which are generally characterized by central power, uniformity, and non-egalitarianism. The Marxist evolutionary model of the authoritarian Left in the Philippines is consistent with this model. To apply this in our context, the indigenous communities "discovered" by Magellan in Leyte were supposedly primitive, inferior, savage, wild, ignorant, and needed to be tamed.

Spain, according to the DHM model, was a feudal society governed by a king. Based on historical accounts, Philip had no intention of conquering the archipelago, it was an enterprise, and he was in business with Magellan. They had a contract that defined each party's obligations and shares.

The word *primitive* is, in most cases, used with prejudice, referring to traditional cultures as underdeveloped. There are hosts of communities that maintained their indigenous ways of life, because they chose to protect and defend their culture by practicing it, by reproducing, innovating, and improving it. They sustained their existence, and not because they were left out of social progression, as presented in the chiefdom model or the dialectical historical tool. Their resilience must be attributed to their love of freedom and self-determination.

Most indigenous communities consciously maintained their cultures. Like any organization, they had mechanisms to protect their well-being by continuously doing things based on their customs and indigenous ways. Like indicators of a healthy ecology, they were highly diverse and their systems myriad. Their commonality was a decentralized pattern of politics and of managing resources. Communities were autonomous and generally had horizontal social relations. The indigenous communities of the archipelago still live according to these principles.

Electricity, gadgets, cars, groceries, malls, appliances, bombs, cannons, nuclear power and arms, churches, guns, and bullets do not exist in the remaining stateless societies. They lack sophisticated technology and material culture in the same way they lack hunger, poverty, crime, ecological destruction, forced labor, different kinds of abuse and exploitation, and social issues attributed to large-scale, centralized power, to authoritarian, consumerist, and patriarchal modern societies.

For sure, indigenous communities are not perfect, but the imperfections are far less destructive than systems of states, corporations, and churches that instigate war, exploitation, environmental destruction, hunger, and poverty through the control of centralized political power. Since the common interest of organisms is to secure their existence, I could say indigenous communities are more developed and advanced, because they are more sustainable than modern

institutions constantly seeking dominance and aiming for infinite growth, which is totally inconsistent with ecological systems and the self-determination of communities.

I have heard several times that what Marx did in his DHM was to interpret history. I agree. But you and me, we can also have our own reading. I would say that the evolutionary approach is not suitable for analyzing our local context. Based on historical accounts, the indigenous organizations did not evolve into states but, rather, were coerced into adopting centralized patterns of organization, such as states, churches, and corporations.

Autonomous/indigenous resistance was the resistance staged by different communities and tribes throughout the archipelago. These were anticolonial in nature and aimed to reinstall their indigenous ways of life. They were led by figures like Magat Salamat, Tamblot, Tapar, Bancao, and others. In the perspective of statists, their initiatives were "primitive."

DHM's hierarchical outlook downplays societies considered part of a "lower" evolutionary process and treats them as underdeveloped and in need of evolving into a higher form. It seems as if poverty, environmental degradation, and social injustice are regarded as prerequisites for the imagined perfect society of the future.

Diversity, horizontality, and spontaneity are the very foundations of life. Life on earth will not flourish through singularity but, rather, through a multitude of systems that are interdependent, directly and indirectly connected to one another. No life on earth is guided by a systematic plan and a singular direction. Life on earth thrives on a process of evolution involving conflict and cooperation.

Our modern age is characterized by centralized politics, an approach that seeks an absolute truth, aiming to establish uniformity and singularity—a framework totally opposed to the foundation of life, i.e., diversity, heterogeneity, and tolerance.

Institutions like states, markets, and churches exist due to a particular objective. They are designed to ensure obedience, submission, and control.

You may observe that we are experiencing environmental destruction, discrimination, war, and exploitation. This is the result of anthropocentrism. Humanity's domination and control over one another and the earth results in the destruction not only of our diverse systems and cultures but also of our very own habitat.

One will notice that the logic of DHM is not only hierarchical but also reinforces uniformity. It is supposed to promote freedom, and many leftist revolutionaries believe this. But its singular and hierarchical direction inevitably discriminates against societies that are not Eurocentric and that oppose systems of industry, market, democracy, and one God–based spirituality. DHM replicates oppressive systems. We have seen this in various places that have adopted Marxism.

PANGAYAW
Decolonizing Resistance in a Network of Communities in the Archipelago (2019)

Introduction

Mutual cooperation is inherent in every human aggregation, a relationship that naturally evolved due to people's biological and social needs.[1] Likewise, the absence of authority and coercion is natural to human relationships. This presupposes that every individual human being can voluntarily act and behave in accordance with the social responsibilities and duties established through actual practices.

This view inevitably leads to the assumption that institutionalized hierarchy is not natural but, rather, human-made, a synthetic relationship that through institutions produces slavery and oppression. Competition has been present in human relationships since time immemorial, but we have mistaken it as a core tool for survival. Under hierarchical frameworks like statism and capitalism, competition is catastrophic, dehumanizing, destructive, corrupting, and unsustainable.

The world population in 10,000 BCE was about ten million. People lived in stateless societies. By the time Columbus reached America, the world population had grown to 350 million, and only one percent was living in non-state societies. Today, only 0.001 percent are living outside of the direct influence of states and other centralized institutions. People in non-state societies are autonomous, they generate their own subsistence with no or very little assistance from the outside world. They bow to no external leaders or authorities. Their lifeways are consistent with ecological processes. As a result of European colonization in the sixteenth century, stateless groups have fallen under the influence of states and mainstream Western society.

Competition is the mainstream framework reinforced by markets, states, and religious institutions through their highly bureaucratic relations. People compete at the top of the hierarchy to achieve the highest privilege and influence. The groups of people at the top of the structure compete to exploit people, communities, and the environment to maintain and increase their benefits and power.

Mainstream societies are characterized by social injustices, poverty, the political marginalization of communities, and ecological crises. In the Philippines, these social conditions have not changed despite several uprisings. Government reports of a 7.3 percent expansion of the economy or a domestic liquidity growth of 16 percent in 2006 or an increase in the balance of payments or other alleged proof of positive economic development cannot conceal the real conditions of millions of hungry, homeless, and landless people living without dignity throughout the archipelago. The techno-fascist jargon is not translatable into concrete gains enjoyed by the people.

This paper is an attempt to contribute to the development of an alternative politics against the hierarchical and centralistic politics that dominate our current social relations, causing slavery, hunger, poverty, discrimination, war, oppression, and ecological destruction. Politics and economy will be treated as strictly interrelated—if one of them remains unfulfilled, the concept of direct democracy will be incomplete. Politics of representation is nothing but elite democracy; as long as centralization of power prevails, democracy will not be realized, because power will naturally fall into the hands of a few representatives. Political participation requires concrete manifestations, such as equitable access to benefit streams and social services.

The effort of understanding the pre-Spanish archipelago is an attempt to explore alternative social setups that were once used by our ancestors. Multiple studies have deepened our appreciation and understanding of the social relations of our ancestors, characterized mainly by mutual cooperation and horizontal political relations.

The word *archipelago* is consistently used to affirm the concept espoused by the "Archipelagic Confederation" article issued and published in 2006. The concept captures the geographical characteristics of a network of cultures and the very essential role of rich but fragile and finite natural resources that have strongly influenced the highly diverse lifestyles of the archipelago's inhabitants. Myriad historical accounts indicate that the bodies of water surrounding the different islands actually connected rather than separated them from each other. The economic, social, and political activities of the inhabitants developed due to the interconnectedness of their immediate environments. The group of islands we call the Philippines today is part of an archipelago that connects the borderless communities of islands and islets in Luzon, the Visayas, Mindanao, Maguindanao, and south to the Talaud Islands, Ternate, Tidore, Halmahera, Borneo, the Moluccas, and as far as Makassar and Brunei. Southeast Asian communities in modern-day Thailand, Sri Lanka, Malaysia, and other places were also part of the traditional network.

The word *autonomous* is consistently used to describe the absence of absolute and centralized power—this means there was no figurehead, whether familial or individual. The themes of diversity and respect were dominant and meant recognition of all communities. The absence of a despotic leader allowed the autonomous character of communities to flourish during ancient times. This also included the autonomy of an individual from their group.

It is erroneous to assume that our ancestors' anarchistic ways of life were perfect; like any culture throughout the world, ours has limitations. But such imperfections are incomparable to the Western campaigns of colonization that caused deep misery for the indigenous communities of Africa, America, and Asia. Their sophisticated methods included genocide, torture, rape, massive destruction of natural resources, slavery, and war in the guise of development, democracy, and freedom.

We have our indigenous concepts of development and freedom, evidence from our prehistoric past, historical documents, and ethnographic studies; they all suggest that our ancestors maintained, sustained, and fought for their freedom and self-determination.

Reconnection to our indigenous past is necessary for us to explore the wisdom of autonomy and ecologically sound ways of living. This wisdom will be used in our current context with the aim of abolishing hunger, poverty, discrimination, patriarchy, war, and control.

Key Words
Archipelago
According to Wikipedia, an archipelago is "a chain, cluster or collection of islands, or sometimes a sea containing a small number of scattered islands. The word *archipelago* is derived from the Greek—*pélagos* ('sea') through the Italian *arcipelago*. In Italian, possibly following a tradition of antiquity, the *Archipelago* was the proper name for the Aegean Sea and, later, usage shifted to refer to the Aegean Islands."

As stated earlier, the word will be used for ecological settings and cultural networks of communities before the advent of the nation-state. It cuts across from Luzon, the Visayas, Mindanao, Sulu, Sarangani, the Talaud Islands, Sangihe, Sulawesi, Borneo, Halmahera, Malacca through Brunei to neighboring communities in Malaysia, Indonesia, Vietnam, Cambodia, and other areas in Southeast Asia that were also directly and indirectly part of relations based on kinship, trade, marriage, and war.

Antiauthoritarian

Wikipedia states that antiauthoritarians believe in full equality before the law and strong civil liberties. Sometimes, the term is used interchangeably with "anarchism," an ideology which entails opposing authority or hierarchical organization, including the state system, in the conduct of human relations.

This document will refer to antiauthoritarian politics as a politics against the centralization of power, which is associated with a leader-centered approach and relevant representation. Usually, leaders and representatives are in authority and possess power used to control and exploit people, communities, organisms, and environments to maintain a status quo that is favorable to a few privileged groups and families.

Autonomous

Webster's New World Thesaurus defines *autonomy* as "liberty, independence and sovereignty." The word will be used for a political belief based on one's self-determination and not accepting the external authority, representation, and centralization espoused by the state, market, and religion. Said political belief encourages independent, free, and critical thinking. It has a deep recognition of cultural diversity and a deep respect for ecology.

As we will discuss later, autonomy mainly relates to the capacity of an individual, a group of people, or a community to make decisions based on actual situations, conditions, and available information, as well as the capacity to implement such decisions.

Decolonization

> Decolonization is the meaningful and active resistance to the forces of colonialism that perpetuate the subjugation and/or exploitation of our minds, bodies, and lands. Its ultimate purpose is to overturn the colonial structure and realize Indigenous liberation. First and foremost,

decolonization must occur in our own minds. The Tunisian decolonization activist, Albert Memmi, wrote, "In order for the colonizer to be the complete master, it is not enough for him to be so in actual fact, he must also believe in its legitimacy. In order for that legitimacy to be complete, it is not enough for the colonized to be a slave, he must also accept his role." The first step toward decolonization, then, is to question the legitimacy of colonization. Once we recognize the truth of this injustice, we can think about ways to resist and challenge colonial institutions and ideologies. Thus, decolonization is not passive, but rather it requires something called praxis.[2]

Anticolonization is the struggle to liberate a particular territory from colonial power and to drive away external authority by establishing another one. In my judgment, the presentation of history where the center subject is the Katipunan is about the founding of a nation-state. But if we focus on the nation-state, it is more about replicating colonial systems rather than cultivating indigenous systems of organization.

Decolonial processes do not tell you to adopt indigenous culture, but they do not stop you from doing so either. The most essential in this process is awareness. If someone takes action it should be their decision.

Direct Democracy

There are plenty of practices and ideas with regard to the notion of direct democracy. In a broad sense, direct democracy will be applied by organizing free associations and assemblies at the local level: people's organizations that are based on communal interests, such as those of peasants, fishers, women, youth, indigenous people, vendors, tricycle drivers, jeepney drivers, the homeless, gays, neighborhood associations, religious groups, and other formations at the local level. They should be encouraged to organize themselves.

These formations will directly participate in public decision-making processes under the theme of mutual cooperation for the benefit of the community rather than competition, which is designed to outcompete, overpower, and control.

Unlike representative democracy, direct democracy is not leader-oriented; it requires direct participation of the most marginalized sectors or individuals through a process of consultation, education, and dialogue based on relevant information and data. It provides venues for the people to speak with regard to their actual situations without any mediation.

Diversity
Diversity is a perfect indicator of a healthy ecology and free communities and people. Differences of cultures, perspectives, values, and lifeways are natural; we are all organically different, and that is our strength. Constant exposure to one another improves our culture. Diversity will not thrive in an authoritarian condition.

Self-determination
According to the *Collins Online Dictionary*, self-determination is "the act or power of making up one's own mind about what

to think or do, without outside influence or compulsion." In this paper, it describes the practice of communities in many different regions of the archipelago, communities that aim to live their lives based on their indigenous views of the world. They have consciously adopted mechanisms to ensure sustenance, development, and improvement of their own culture collectively through mutual cooperation.

It should be emphasized that these words, ideas, and concepts are based on actual practices that are directly related to one another and used interchangeably.

Systematic Hunger and Poverty

It is reasonable to consider that industrial revolution eliminated the threat of scarcity of foods and other necessary things, making it, in theory, possible for everyone to live comfortably. State-of-the-art technology never ceased to evolve. Given the current state of technology, it is safe to conclude that we have already created highly efficient means to produce foods and other necessities for our daily lives.

In fact, one of the core issues in multilateral and bilateral trade negotiations is market access. Capitalist nations and transnational corporations are looking for markets where they can dump their huge surpluses. Trade-related issues may appear complicated. At the World Trade Organization (WTO), for instance, the negotiations about Non-Agricultural Market Access (NAMA) produced too complex a formula to balance the interests of players. Nonetheless, the aim is to reduce tariffs at a substantial rate, and the ultimate goal is elimination. But tariff elimination will lead to the demise of the local economy and local livelihoods due to incompetent local industries and sectors that become more vulnerable due to a lack of or absence of subsidies.

We do not aim to simplify trade discourse, but we must not let tricky words and concepts revolving around trade issues deceive us. Developed and developing countries alike, especially the US, EU, Japan, and China, as well as others, cannot conceal their intention to expand their markets to allow their corporations to make more profit. Investments are among the critical issues being discussed to access the Third World's remaining natural resources. These facts make one thing obvious: the threat of underproduction and scarcity has long been addressed and totally eliminated. Yet poverty and hunger still persist at the global scale.

The great volume of products, both agricultural and industrial, moving freely at the global scale correspond to the volume of profit created in the process. Meanwhile, a great number of people are starving on a daily basis, especially in the developing and poor nations, which have high figures of impoverished children, women, small producers (peasants and fishers), workers from rural areas, and urban poor. The current situation denies them access to basic things, such as food, clothing, shelter, water, education, health services, and the opportunity for a sustainable livelihood.

The Social Weather Stations' survey results of the fourth quarter of 2014 estimated that 11.4 million families in the Philippines considered themselves poor.[3] Do you have any idea how it is to live on less than one dollar a day? Meanwhile, the few who have access to power and influence over the economy live their lives luxuriously and extravagantly.

Over ten million Filipinos go hungry every year. The latest record puts the number of unemployed and under-employed people at about 4.5 million. Every year, almost one million women and men want to leave the country to seek job opportunities. The country has one of the largest numbers of malnourished children in the world. In 2000, the country ranked 77 out of more than 150 countries, with a poverty incidence of 34 percent. The human development index (HDI) figure was 0.656. Eighty percent of fisher households lived below the poverty line.[4]

Poverty becomes a complicated issue when experts start to raise opinions. If there is a single explanation, it would be social inequality. There is no need for rocket science to comprehend the relationship between the rich and the have-nots. The gap between them is big enough to stare right at the reality of inequality.

Basic logic and mathematics will lead us to the reality that vast productive lands and resources are controlled and occupied by only a few families. This results in the misery of millions of landless farmers. The business of a few influential families who accumulate massive profits continuously expands the gap between the rich and the poor. The same group of people will likely have superior access to the economy due to its influence in decision-making. Public services that could have helped reduce the burden of the poor majority are rarely accessible to common people.

One of the core problems is one that we do not need a genius to comprehend: the privatization of our finite, exhaustible, and limited resources. This inevitably results in marginalization and poverty for millions of people.

Democracy Scandal

The current political setup has created confusion with regard to the meaning and concept of the word *democracy*. What is taught in schools, textbooks, and formal documents is far from the actual practice of democracy.

The fall of the monarchs in France in 1789 ended the idea that "some people are born to rule." Moreover, it was followed shortly after by the downfall of many powerful monarchies in Europe. The ideas of equality and individual rights were expressed and legally adopted by the revolutionary National Assembly in the *Declaration of the Rights of Man and Citizen*.

The monarchies collapsed; the merchants and the bourgeoisie rose, cleverly inventing the idea of democracy to maintain hegemony and their privilege and to protect the capitalist setup of a private-property regime.

The neoliberal paradigm is one of the most effective tools of capitalism. It created institutions like the International Monetary Fund-World Bank (IMF-WB) and the WTO.

Agreements signed by the Philippines, including ASEAN (Association of Southeast Asian Nations), RP (Republic of the Philippines)-China, ASEAN-China, and JPEPA (Japan-Philippine Economic Partnership Agreement), are among the agreements where the agenda of the neoliberals is being pushed.

The economic assistance offered by IMF-WB makes many communities pay a very dear price. In exchange for loans, the Philippine government legislates policies to implement privatization and liberalization based on Structural Adjustment Programs (SAPs). With the coercive assistance from IMF-WB, privatization and liberalization are imposed on poor and developing countries like ours. Privatization dispossesses, marginalizes, and displaces communities of farmers, fishers, indigenous groups, and women.

In practice, the capitalist system and the neoliberal paradigm are inconsistent with the idea of democracy. Ideally, democracy is defined as a system wherein all people in a particular territory or community directly partake in decision-making. However, the elites and corporations that control the means of production will not allow workers to participate, because they are just part of machines that produce commodities. Direct-democratic decision-making is a great threat to profits, property, and privileges. In many cases, workers participate through unions, but the results—for example, collective bargaining agreements—are limited and do not really secure substantial gains.

Democracy is a political system developed as an alternative to the absolute control by the monarchs over all social and economic affairs. This is supposed to provide not only political freedom but also freedom to access benefit streams and social services.

After a long coercive process of colonization, the archipelago finally became an independent republic based on a constitution upholding democratic principles. In practice, our political system of making decisions and implementing them,

described as democracy, is divided into three major institutions. The legislature enacts laws through the congress and the senate. The judiciary interprets laws. Finally, the executive implements policies led by the president and aided by a bunch of secretaries through huge bureaucracies of departments and line agencies. The police and the military deal with those who stubbornly resist. In theory, these three branches of government have equal power, but in many cases the executive branches exercise overwhelming influence.

Generally, most of the decisions made by "honorable" lawmakers are totally opposed to people's interests. For instance, the government's lousy alibi on E-VAT is fiscal deficit. This is highly doubtful. Let us assume that the situation is real. During the time of Jose Isidro Camacho, formerly a minister of energy as well as finance, the Bureau of Internal Revenue admitted that the institution is inefficient in terms of collecting government revenues; this inefficiency cost the government losses of as much as 40 percent. Included in these are uncollected revenues due to tax evasion by big businesses, smuggling of various products, and, not least, the government's virtual removal of tariffs and the provisions of tax holidays for foreign and local corporations. How did intelligent officials, lawmakers, experts, and doctors in economics miss these facts? Did they run out of brains and turn to people's pockets, not even bothering to rethink the huge amount that goes to useless government debt and loan payments due to automatic appropriation laws?

During Gloria Macapagal Arroyo's administration, she had the power to veto the bill submitted by the legislature. But she herself, as an economist, failed to see the objective conditions and let her government collect E-VAT (12 percent) for every processed product bought, including non-nutrient instant noodles, one of the most affordable food products for millions of poor families.

Going back to the trade liberalization issue, let's say we agree to compete and combine with industrious and creative men and women who can establish great competitive advantage in the agriculture and fishery sectors. Again, the government missed these simple facts and decided to open up our sensitive sectors. Worse, it encouraged foreign investors to exploit our rich mineral and energy resources without clear long-term gains for the communities where the project sites are located. News networks do not run out of news about the violations and abuses of investors in tourism, logging, fishing, natural gas extraction, mineral resources exploitation, and others.

While liberalizing sensitive sectors, leaders made a policy that prohibited the import of cheap drugs and medicines. Because of this, the archipelago has the highest price for medicines in Southeast Asia. They are inaccessible to poor people.

In a democratic system, everyone is entitled to offer their services to the public. If someone wishes to run for office, let's say in a *barangay*, they must be ready to spend one hundred thousand to one million pesos in order to effectively reach the voters (the cost varies based on the size of the barangay). If someone is seeking the office of House of Representative, they must have a minimum of a million pesos for the campaign. During the senatorial race of 2007, for example, GMA 7 reported that at the beginning of the campaign candidates like Prospero Pichay and Ralph Recto had already spent twenty million pesos for TV advertisements alone. The fact is that government offices are expensive and accessible only to the few who have capital and influence. One will conclude that these offices are lucrative businesses under the guise of service and patriotism.

That is why it is not surprising that the political leaders of today are the same families who have held office since the Spaniards left. They used the same old catchphrases, such as "change," "democracy," "development," "pro-people," "pro-god," and "pro-environment," to make themselves appear worthy of their office, but the trick is that they are the same few families who own and control the economic, political, and cultural institutions of the country.

This is what democracy looks like.

A Shortsighted Sense of History

In order to be able to imagine our ancestors' lives and to comprehend indigenous lifeways to learn from their wisdom, this paper utilizes a multitude of ideas emanated from multiple disciplines, including anthropology, archeology, history, sociology, and folklore.

The "band-tribe-chiefdom-state" model of analyzing sociocultural complexity pioneered by archaeologist Elman Service refers to a hierarchical progression of society. It presents the evolutionary process of a community from a simple stateless egalitarian indigenous organization like a band or tribe to chiefdoms and states, which are generally characterized by central power, uniformity, and non-egalitarianism. The Marxist evolutionary model of the authoritarian Left in the Philippines is consistent with this model, except that it added the twist of Maoism and concluded that the current state of the Philippine society was semicolonial and semifeudal. Criticism of the chiefdom model is prevalent among scholars in related fields of study. Joyce C. White of the University of Pennsylvania, for instance, argues that this model cannot account for the sociopolitical dynamics of communities in Southeast Asia.[5]

The abovementioned model has readily defined a phase of progression and an established pattern of movement; it is meant to help observers predict the outcome of the process. Most Marxists are inclined to this mode of thinking. The semicolonial/semifeudal analysis is based on dialectical materialism, which presents the hierarchical progression of society consistent to the chiefdom model. The word "primitive," as espoused in dialectical historical frameworks, is used to describe "outmoded" and inferior systems that are expected to improve as time progresses. The first stage will be slavery, followed by feudalism, then capitalism, and so on. If this is the case, is it proper to assume that the centralization of political power, the privatization of benefit streams, ecological crises, hunger, poverty, slavery, and other social issues are requirements to attain the perfect society, which is the communist stage?

The word *primitive*, in most cases, is used with prejudice to refer to traditional cultures as underdeveloped. The indigenous communities still exist, because they chose to protect and defend their culture by practicing it, by reproducing and improving it. *They were not left behind by social progression as presented in the chiefdom model or by the dialectical historical tool. Their resilience is attributed to their love of freedom and self-determination.* Most indigenous communities consciously maintained their culture. Like all organizations, they have mechanisms to protect their well-being by continuously doing things the way they see fit. Electricity, gadgets, cars, groceries, malls, appliances, bombs, cannons, nuclear power, churches, guns, and bullets do not exist in remaining stateless societies. They lack sophisticated technology and material culture the same way they lack hunger, malnutrition, coercion, ecological destruction, forced labor, and social issues attributed to large-scale, centralistic forms of power and to authoritarian, consumerist, and patriarchal modern societies.

Mainstream society has programs to integrate indigenous communities: churches, schools, and corporations are among the institutions that are consistently pestering them. The fact that there are indigenous groups that stand their ground and protect their culture the way their ancestors did during Spanish colonization shows that the evolutionary approach is not suitable to analyze our local context. The indigenous communities throughout the archipelago are highly diverse; there is a multitude of cultural patterns that overlap and consistently influence each other through the process of interaction and exposure. Based on historical accounts, the indigenous organizations did not evolve into states but, rather, were coerced to adopt centralistic patterns of organization, such as states and corporations.

Who Discovered the Philippines?

This is a novelty question in Philippine mainstream society; it is usually asked if one wants to joke during history-related conversations. The answer reveals one's wittiness—or historical shortsightedness.

Nowadays, people's sense of history revolves around the idea of Spanish colonization and the Katipunan uprising, which led to the establishment of a republic. This was a historical period that connected many communities in the archipelago to the modern setting dominated by nation-states and characterized by centralized social relations and absolute truths along with poverty, hunger, injustice, discrimination, and ecological destruction.

Spain is perceived as the villain that brought suffering to the people; it is also considered as a "master" who introduced the idea of a civilized life. Since civilization is viewed as the benchmark of development, it is considered plausible to think that we owe Spain our progress.

Mainstream history is Eurocentric. It will inevitably treat pre-Spanish cultures and lifestyles as underdeveloped, as savages and backwoodsmen that needed to be changed according to the standards of the colonizers.

This is exactly where we are now. We challenge the negative attributes of the society introduced by the colonizers, while invoking alternatives which were also introduced by colonizers.

For instance, the Katipunan challenged Spanish authority by asserting its capacity to self-rule through the system introduced by colonizers. Revolutionary ideas carried by anti-colonialism are Western in origin.

In mainstream terms, Philippine history exclusively refers to the period where written documentation is involved. The year 1521 is recognized by mainstream society as the year of the so-called discovery of the Philippines.

The novelty question is being asked constantly and spontaneously perhaps because our history is haunting us. *The terms* Philippines *and* Filipino *are not ours. They were imposed on us by the colonizers and coercively used to describe and define us. They are the very attributes that reinforced the disconnection from our indigenous selves.* They make us think that we are superior to other cultures. Why the need for superiority? Is it to defeat and outcompete other people and to undermine their cultural orientation?

Our own culture should be our guide in our search for self-determination. Our self-determination is no justification to control or to coerce others. Our ancestors' system displays no center. They never had uniform conduct that exercised control. What they had were diverse cultural orientations that cut across the archipelago and into Southeast Asia, facilitated by marriage, kinship, trade, and war.

We are not Filipinos. We are people raised by diverse cultures. Our culture is a gift from our ancestors. It is not perfect, but it has the complete set of elements under the theme of mutual cooperation and respect.

There is no such thing as a "perfect culture." But ours is far more humane and ecologically sound than the nation-state and capitalism, systems that introduced massive killings of people, the destruction of culture, and the destruction of the earth. There is no one big formula that could provide a single solution to the problems we are currently facing, but at least we have the wisdom from our ancestors providing us with a framework that has proven to be effective and is still utilized by indigenous cultures across the archipelago.

Lapu-Lapu's victory over Ferdinand Magellan in 1521 is iconic. The message it conveyed was not about a nation and sovereignty. It was about the defense of the autonomy of Mactan Island. Numerous forms of resistance followed the struggle, aiming to reinstitute the indigenous setup in order to protect people's autonomy.

The fragmentation of cultural communities should not be viewed as weakness. It represents freedom and autonomy. These communities have indigenous means to connect and integrate; fragmentation is only a weakness if one has the intention to control and dominate.

Various communities throughout the archipelago have been in existence since time immemorial. The earliest traces of prehistoric humans and their tools are found in Palawan in a group of caves called Tabon Caves, located at the mouth of the South China Sea. Tools from different periods in pre-history have been dug up at these sites. How long ago the tools were used or how long ago the humans and animals whose traces have been found lived is learned through a complex process of analyzing the findings. Excavations in the Tabon Caves have revealed fossils of prehistoric animals (elephants, giant tortoises, and others) along with artifacts that have left traces of human inhabitation. Chert and choppers made of hard stone were recovered with human and animal bones scattered in the surroundings. Based on these fossils, archaeologists have estimated that humans occupied the caves as early as fifty thousand years ago.

Experts and scholars will not cease to amaze with the volume of artifacts recovered in different places in the archipelago that provide clues of the wisdom of our ancestors. Archaeologists believe that at the end of the glacial period, that is about 10,000 BCE, human dispersal across half of the planet began from Burma (Myanmar) and the south coast of mainland China. This particular stock belongs to Malayo-Polynesian or Austronesian cultures believed to be our ancestors, and to those of the Malaysians, Indonesians, and Polynesians. These peoples are considered the first boat people of human history, highly mobile in that borderless part of Asia. It is said that before the Phoenicians roamed the Mediterranean with their wooden ships, our ancestors had already tamed the violent and treacherous waves of the Pacific and successfully reached islands, such as Fiji, Samoa, and Hawaii, with tiny makeshift boats we call *balanghay*. Therefore, we have a deep and meaningful base of cultural identity that cannot be erased by the culture of consumerism and authoritarian politics of colonialism reinforced by the state, religion, and market institutions.

As mentioned above, the group of islands we today call the Philippines is part of the archipelago that connects the borderless communities of islands and islets in Luzon, the Visayas, Mindanao, Maguindanao, and to the south, including the Talaud Islands, Ternate, Tidore, Halmahera, the Moluccas, Borneo, and as far as Makassar and Brunei. We also have indigenous connections in Thailand, Indonesia, Sri Lanka, Malaysia, and other southeast Asian societies. What we had was a highly diverse culture, a culture that was inherited by remaining indigenous communities and deposited to folklore transmitted through oral tradition. We have ancient historical roots, a rhizome of complex cultures deeply crisscrossing the upland, misty rainforests and river systems and lakes freely reaching to bays, gulfs, and coves connected to the Celebes Sea, the Sulu Sea, and up in the South China Sea.

The 1521 incident, when Lapu-Lapu defeated Magellan, marked a milestone in the resistance against the West intending to control us. Our ancestors roamed in borderless seas, rivers, and lakes. Our culture cannot be contained within the boundary set by the Treaty of Tordesillas.[6] The treaty cannot limit the movements, interactions, and relationships of the diverse cultures of our ancestors. *The "Philippines" symbolize the acceptance and submission to the concept of development, politics, and culture of the West. It is a disconnection from our indigenous selves.*

Nowadays, indigenous groups and their practices are neglected due to the dominance of Western ideologies in all aspects of our lives. This situation has, in most cases, reduced them to subjects of ridicule, and we failed to explore the wisdom inherent in their practices that is more meaningful than the framework and alternative crafted by the intellectuals and cultures from the West. The intention of this document is to reinforce and support what existed prior to the creation of the nation-state. Our ancestors were better off and lived in freedom, to its closest proximity.

Pangayaw as a Process in Decolonizing Our Well-Being

Colonization generally refers to the process that is perpetuated after the initial control over Indigenous Peoples is achieved through invasion and conquest. Perpetuating colonization allows the colonizers to maintain or expand their social, political, and economic power. It is detrimental to us because their power comes at the expense of Indigenous lands, resources, lives, and self-determination. Not only has colonization resulted in the loss of major rights such as land and self-determination, most of our contemporary daily struggles are also a direct consequence of colonization (poverty, family violence, chemical dependency, suicide, health deterioration). Colonization is an all-encompassing presence in our lives.[7]

This definition is from the book *For Indigenous Minds Only.* In my own understanding, colonialization is the complete acceptance of an external culture and authority which leads to the denial of one's indigenous self, identity, and community. An obvious fact is the current modes of thinking of mainstream culture, in which the superior practices and frameworks are Western. This concerns language, food, drugs, music, politics, education, and beliefs. Almost all aspects of our lives are highly influenced by centralized and absolute truths, as well as by uniformity.

I know that many of us are hell-bent in terms of addressing social issues that affect our very own families and households—social issues that were introduced in connection with colonialization. Since Western thinking is deeply inculcated in us, even the very alternatives we employ are derived from external authorities. We tend to turn to the idea of democracy, sovereignty, development, socialism, GNP, GDP, and progress rather than the wisdom and practices we inherited from our ancestors.

With the adverse impacts and bad results of statist socialist and authoritarian leftists, communities and social movements inevitably seek viable and sustainable systems to protect and maintain our households and communities.

None of us would disagree with the fact that we have our own set of systems. Systems that colonization, by Westerners and Asians alike, tried to eliminate. These indigenous systems refuse to give up; they maintain their existence. The remaining cultural communities owe their resilience to the continuous practice and improvement of indigenous systems. These are sustainable systems being subjected by mainstream society to ridicule and marginalization. Mainstream and centralized institutions, such as states, corporations, and churches, are set to eliminate them by intensifying mining and logging activities and building schools and religious structures within territories of indigenous communities.

In the midst of absolutism, authoritarianism, anthropocentrism, and intolerance to diversity, our indigenous roots are the remaining unexplored alternatives. *Pangayaw* was the practice of our ancestors most feared by the colonizers. They had every reason to eliminate pangayaw due to its efficiency in countering early attempts of colonization. Pangayaw is an act of raiding, on land or on sea. The reason could be revenge, unsettled disputes, or simply the desire to loot and capture slaves. The raiders of the Visayans were among those most feared, their notoriety reaching all the way to communities in southern China. Major languages within the archipelago use the word *pangayaw* to refer to this activity. Historian William Henry Scott noted that it was an accepted practice.

In my current mode of thinking and values, I will definitely go against this practice. Why would I support such acts of atrocity? Such practices are totally opposite to the culture that raised me. But an attempt to understand our ancestors' culture will require us to suspend our judgment influenced by the standards of mainstream society. I would be inclined to disagree if one were to consider pangayaw as wrong and evil, because, in the end, it is no different from the policy of Spain, which set out to eliminate our ancestors' culture, including tattooing, the defiling of teeth, earlobes, body piercings, g-strings, and so forth. If one insists on the barbarity of pangayaw, I ask in return: How barbarous were the colonizers when they robbed and stole our lands? When they raped and killed our people and destroyed our natural resources?

The practice of pangayaw was a major obstacle to Spanish conquest. One of the early colonies of the Spaniards was the Visayans. With the allegiance of the Visayans to Spain, they were particularly targeted, and there was a prohibition of arms in Cebu and in Bohol. The long-lasting Moro Wars significantly depopulated communities in the Visayas.

It is probable that many of us agree with the objective of making our world better. I would directly equate the term *better* with social justice, ecological sustainability, equal access to services for all, respect, love, and peaceful coexistence. Our common experience tells us that we cannot achieve a better world if we allow control, uniformity, centralism, competition, and absolutism in our different aspects of life.

Pangayaw is an unexplored alternative to commence decolonization. If one were to take me as literally advocating pangayaw, one would conclude that I advocate violence.

Waziyatawin and Michael Yellow Bird note the following:

Scott DeMuth begins chapter 6, "Colonization Is Always War," by describing how any Indigenous challenges to state authority today, even peaceful challenges, are met with threats of police violence, arrests, and heavy surveillance. This serves as a useful reminder to Indigenous people who have come to believe that because we do not observe open repression on a daily basis, we have made progress in our relationships with our colonizers, or that colonization at its core is not still serving the same purpose it always has. DeMuth asserts that because colonization is inherently a war for territory and resources, "If colonization continues today, then it follows that war continues to be waged against Indigenous Peoples and territories." In this context, it is imperative that Indigenous people develop a proper response to warfare, requiring the development of an organized resistance movement. Rather than viewing a potential resistance movement as an offensive action, however, DeMuth points out that decolonization is actually a self-defensive action against the war that is colonization.[8]

Perhaps it is not easy to figure out the direct relationship of colonization to the daily lives of the people, especially if most poor people are busy seeking jobs or livelihood opportunities. The majority of the people would not immediately suspect that colonization is a very effective means of control to maintain inequality in society and ignorance among the people. This situation means war against our very selves. Super-institutions are well equipped in terms of propagating and maintaining legitimacy of inequality, ecological destruction, and the assault on cultural communities through formal processes of the law. Homelessness, hunger, war, and ecological terrorism are accepted social facts that are generally the results of activities of super-institutions.

The process of decolonization is not uniform. It appears and exists in many forms but should start within ourselves, within our families and communities. It is a process that can respond to the immediate impact of macro-events like poverty and ignorance, while strategically laying foundations of future alternatives through increasing awareness of our indigenous roots.

Communities, households, associations, and other formations at the local and grassroots level, particularly if they operate in nonauthoritarian processes, will never run out of ideas and creativity. Decolonial processes are no blueprint and do not follow standardized conduct; they offer diverse methods and actions but won't reinforce and promote authoritarianism, absolutism, and hierarchy. Indigenous systems and traditions are banks of information; they offer multitudes of practices that facilitate the improvement of our consciousness and lifeways toward claiming our self-determination.

To engage in decolonization means to engage in war. Our age is the age of the propaganda war. We can use pangayaw to engage in a propaganda war against centralized institutions. Direct action always delivers strong messages; it's an effective means of propaganda that sends a message of sharing, respect, love, ecology, social justice, and self-determination.

Solidarity actions to uplift the spirit of autonomous resistance and to support independent movements and communities through the sharing of skills, resources, and knowledge are concrete activities that would definitely hit hierarchy at its core.

Overall, our activities toward decolonialization will establish the reconnection to our indigenous roots.

Historical Notes on Decolonial Events

The historical victory of Lapu-Lapu was temporal and just the beginning of autonomous resistance that plagued 333 years of Spanish occupation. The resistance became more intense in 1581, when Friar Andres Aguirre implemented the policy of gathering locals in order to teach indigenous communities to live in a "civilized" and European way.

In 1587, Tagalog leaders set up a conspiracy to topple Spanish rule, where the primary objective was to regain the privileges they had lost. They wanted to collect taxes for themselves rather than the Spaniards, and they wanted the return of their slaves and women, whom the friars had freed and sent back home. The group of leaders who conspired were Magat Salamat, the son of Rajah Matanda, from Tondo, Pedro Balinguit from Pandacan, Felipe Amarlangagui from Catangalan, Omaghicon from Navotas, Felipe Salonga from Polo, in Bulacan, his brother Dionisio Capolo from Candaba, in Pampanga, and Pitongatan, Joan Banal, and other members of the feudal *maharlika* class from Tondo. Salamat particularly demanded the reestablishment of the *datu* regime.[9]

The revolt was well-planned but never executed due to the betrayal of Antonio Surabao, a Tagalog who happened to be employed by the Spanish captain Pedro Sarmiento. On November 4, 1588, Governor De Vera ordered the arrest of all the leaders of the conspiracy.

According to the account *The Philippine Islands, 1493–1898, Volume XXIII, 1629–30*,[10] eight years after Rajah Sulayman and Rajah Matanda fell from power, Maynila (now Manila) came under the control of the Spaniards. The colonizers went to the town of Li Han (now Malolos) and conquered four thousand residents. The following years, there were sporadic revolts around the area that would later be called Bulacan, but this was not sustained until 1643, when a Bornean, Pedro Ladia, came and convinced the Bulakenyos to turn their backs on the Spaniards. He claimed that he was the Rajah of Tagalog and was supposed to inherit Rajah Matanda's throne. He insisted on reinstituting traditional practices, such as the belief in local spirits and deities like *bathala*, *anyito*, and *diwata*. The Augustinian priest Cristóbal Enríquez discovered Ladia's plot. Ladia was secretly arrested and transferred to Manila to be executed.

In 1621, Tamblot, a traditional priest from the province of Bohol, preached traditional beliefs. He told people that it was about time to abandon foreign religion; diwata, anyito, and the spirits of their ancestors would provide them with food and protect them from the Spaniards. His followers went into hiding in the forest, where they built a holy place of their own and performed their traditional rites. Tamblot's teachings spread like wildfire due to the organizers he had strategically deployed on the entire island. Many Boholanos joined the barangay he established in the heart of the forest. The Jesuit priests, who were powerful on the island at that time, did, of course, condemn what they were doing. Tamblot and two thousand followers revolted. They burned down all the churches and statues of saints on the entire island, except for Loboc and Baclayon. The Jesuits went to Cebu and told Alcalde Mayor Juan Alcarazo about the revolt. Alcarazo knew that Cebuanos would not fight Boholanos and waited for one hundred Pampango soldiers to come from Manila. He also recruited a thousand people from Sialo and fifty homeless Spaniards.

On January 1, 1622, four outrigger warships went ashore to suppress Tamblot. The first attack made Tamblot retreat and establish another camp. The second encampment did not last due to serious losses inflicted during the first attack. The rebels ran out of arrows and so the battle was bolo knives and stones against guns. As expected, Tamblot's revolt failed.

The Babaylan had already been in fifty years of hiding when the Spanish took control of the archipelago. The

Spanish were alerted by Tamblot's revolt and began chasing them again actively. On the island of Leyte, the seventy-year-old Bancao established a barangay in Carigara, similar to the one in Bohol. The Waray-Waray were prepared to revolt and waited for results from Bohol. In late 1622, after almost a year of waiting, Bancao's group started the uprising. They burned no churches and destroyed no Christian symbols, but they denounced Spaniards and their teachings. The churches were emptied and the locals stopped rendering services to the friars.

Friar Melchor de Vera went to Cebu and asked assistance from Juan Alcarazo. He brought his soldiers to Leyte and, with the help of locals, discovered Bancao's whereabouts. Alcarazo divided his forces into three and attacked the barangay from various sides; the many guns of the Spanish forces overwhelmed Bancao's warriors. The Waray-Waray fled to the forests; children and women in traditional Babaylan wardrobe were killed by soldiers upon the orders of the priests.

Mang Abu was a known leader in 1629 in Caraga. It was a time when Davao del Sur and Davao del Norte still belonged to Caraga. The rebellion was started when Mang Abu confronted Spanish soldiers who were involved in the illegal business of capturing locals for the slave trade. He was mauled by a captain, assisted by twenty soldiers, when he asked them to free the Tagabaloys and Mandayas.

Mang Abu asked the people why they let foreigners harm their peers. They were superior in numbers, and Mang Abu was conscious of this advantage. He convinced the locals to act immediately. They chased out the Spanish troops, killed them all, including the priest, and then freed all the locals.

Conscious of the danger of retaliation, the Mandayas urged the indigenous groups to kill all Spaniards in the village of Basuag. The Mandayas attacked the Spanish fortress, but the Spaniards had already been warned and had closed all possible entries. The Mandayas decided to lock them in. Hundreds of boats surrounded the Spanish fort in Tandag to intercept all possible help. The Spaniards were terrified. They did not have sufficient capabilities to fight the Mandayas, and their supply of food was not enough to hold them standing until reinforcements arrived.

The news reached Cebu. The Alcalde mayor was Friar Jacinto de San Fulgencio. He informed Manila about the attacks, and then he assembled a fleet commanded by Capitan Juan de Chaves, an *encomendero* from Caraga.[11] The rebellion was suppressed, and the leaders brutally punished, but Mang Abu was pardoned due to the support from his friar friends.

Similar resistance took place in other places: in Pangasinan and Pampanga in 1660; in Iloilo in 1663; in Bohol in 1744; in Ilocos Norte in 1807. All these revolts were to defend the autonomy of the local communities. Betrayal caused serious damage to most of the resistance, which contributed to its failure. This is because the colonizers were able to penetrate the indigenous political structure. Through blood compacts with the local leaders, the Spaniards were able to exploit their loyalty. They were also able to capture the deeply spiritual locals, using Christianity to control and pacify resistance.

Some have called these uprisings "pocket resistance," revolts intended to reclaim communities' self-determination, which had been undermined by the centralized and authoritarian system. Obviously, they did not stage revolts to establish systems similar to monarchies or republics. Their intention was to regain their indigenous lifeways and to protect their cultures from exploitation by the colonizers.

Our experience tells us that an effort of a community to resist is futile if it is disconnected from other communities that are cooperating with the oppressors. This is perhaps one of the reasons why some considered the Katipunan as the culmination of the resistance. It is plausible to conclude that the Katipunan was the "aggregation" of experience of exploitation and resistance of diverse communities in the archipelago. This aggregation represents common sentiments reinforced by the will to expel Spaniards and to claim sovereignty. Thus, it established a basis of unity among dissenters through the process of representation. A system learned by the local elite from the exploiters and colonizers.

The lens to be used in interpreting the best available data with regard to "our history" is imperative. Representative systems will not work in a highly diverse context, particularly for those communities who practice autonomy. Republicanism is an idea adopted by the few educated people from the privileged section of society dominated by Luzon-based activists, particularly of Tagalogs. It was the second attempt to claim the archipelago under one uniform system after the regalian doctrine introduced by Spain, a treacherous and pretentious claim that would inevitably misrepresent the communities that are not amenable to statism, civilization, uniformity, and authoritarianism.

I do not question the integrity and commitment of our ancestors who fought against the colonizers and oppressors, but adopting the system that was supposed to be overthrown was tantamount to replicating oppression.

The idea of sovereignty through self-governance could have been a tactic to consolidate the locals, while winning support from the international community. The flourishing modernist ideas from the West, such as nationalism, reinforced statist thinking among the locals. It had reached the minds of the likes of Rizal, Aguinaldo, Mabini, Jaena, and del Pilar. Retelling what had been told, Bonifacio, unlike his contemporaries, saw no hope in diplomatic processes. For him, establishing an independent state (republic) required war.

In 1896, the uprising of the Katipunan broke out, but prior to this, Isabelo de los Reyes was arrested. He was not part of any revolutionary group during that time, but his name consistently appeared in newspapers attacking the colonial administration. An activist from the countryside (Ilocos region), he was a journalist, a profession which gave him the opportunity to plant his revolutionary ideas effectively. After he was freed, he wrote a letter calling people to take up arms and launch a guerrilla war, a letter adopted and issued by the Katipunan as an official communiqué signed by Emilio Aguinaldo, as president.

Isabelo was rearrested, and this time he was sent to the prison of Montjuic in Barcelona—a grave mistake by Spanish authorities, because he got connected to various radical people including anarchists. Spain at that time was already highly influenced by anarchism. A few years earlier, Bakunin's comrade Guiseppe Fanneli had gone to Spain to organize workers, and, after several years, workers grasped a profound understanding of anarcho-syndicalism. While José Rizal, considered a national hero by the Philippine Republic, went to universities in Europe, Isabelo joined workers in the streets and learned the anarcho-syndicalist ways.

Spain backed down when Americans asserted their interest over Cuba and the Philippines. In 1901, during this early phase of colonization by the US and the emerging economic order, Isabelo de los Reyes arrived from exile in Spain. Fresh from exposure to anarcho-syndicalism, he introduced an anti-imperialist mode to the resistance. To the amazement of the American capitalists and the local elite, Isabelo was able to mobilize thousands of workers and urban poor in Manila and its surrounding communities. The anti-imperialist resistance was able to organize the Unión Obrera Democrática (UOD), the very first labor union in the so-called Republic of the Philippines. Its basic documents were derived from Pierre-Joseph Proudhon, an anarchist, but the union did not last very long.

The authoritarian Left started to gain influence during the 1930s, and later dominated the radical movement in the archipelago. The Marxists-Leninist ideology of the Bolsheviks proliferated, and its adherents became one of the armed elements that resisted Japanese occupation during World War II. During the 1960s, the Maoists took the steering wheel. Jose Maria Sison's group veered away from the insurrectionary methods of the Bolsheviks and held on to the "protracted people's war": a guerrilla tactic that had raised Mao Zedong to unprecedented popularity during the peasant revolution in China. Sison's group later merged with armed rebels to establish the armed component of the Communist Party of the Philippines (CPP), the New People's Army (NPA). Both became part of the National Democratic Front (NDF).

CPP-NPA-NDF became the most influential within the leftist blocs during the 1970s and up to the latter part of the 1980s. In the 1990s, the dominant leftist formation suffered a crisis that inflicted serious damage on the mass movement. It initially emerged as a question of tactics, and later developed into ideological struggle, becoming the basis of a split that started the fragmentation process and decrease of popularity and influence of the leftist movement.

From early nationalist resistance up to now, whether people advocated arms or education, there was just a difference in tactics, not in objectives; they were all for the creation of centralized political systems with centralized power.

Exchange, Sharing, and Debt: The Autonomous Communities and Indigenous Social Stratification

According to ethnographic accounts by the early Spanish chroniclers, a small barangay was composed of communities with thirty to one hundred households. The biggest were found in Sulu, Butuan, Cebu, Panay, Batangas, Bicol, and Manila, with populations ranging from two thousand to twenty thousand.

Human communities have existed and thrived in different places in the world, with varied social arrangements developed from their interactions with one another, their direct utilization patterns, and the management of natural resources. The social stratification of the communities of the prehistoric archipelago was not uniform, as presented earlier. Communities had their similarities, peculiarities, and variations. The purpose of the discussion with regard to rankings, particularly of Tagalog culture, which shares features with Visayan and Central Luzon traditions and customs, is to be understood in this context. We are used to viewing "slavery" in the context of the European experience, which may not be applicable to our indigenous context and situation. Our indigenous setup has its peculiarities that do not surface if we use conventional analytical thinking.

The practice of sharing and a culture of exchange are imperative when it comes to analyzing society. The processes of exchange and sharing bring significant influence to the relationships of individuals, organizations, and institutions.

Nowadays, economics is a recognized field of study with a special interest in exchange. For many economists, long before money was invented, there was barter: a system of exchange that entailed the swapping of things. In our modern age, money is the most efficient means of exchange, generally adopted by the majority of societies in the world. Anthropologist David Graeber's critique of barter is intriguing. Economists would surely raise their eyebrows, as an anthropologist makes incisive comments on economic discourse.[12] Anyway, the idea of barter, as discussed by the moral philosophy professor Adam Smith in the book *The Wealth of the Nations*, started with the premise that exchange is a behavior exclusive to humans. Humans, if left to their own devices, will exchange and compare things. To reinforce his claim, he described North America where, according to him, indigenous people were engaged in the process of barter. How does barter work? First is the idea of double coincidence, without which barter will not take place. How does double coincidence work? A person, for instance, who has no use for her bike may wish to dispose of it in exchange for a juicer. She needs to find a person who has a juicer to dispose of and needs a bike in exchange. There are two persons who are willing to exchange their items. If their transaction works out, both will dispose of the respective things they don't have use for and acquire new things that satisfy their needs.

However, many centuries have passed, and this land of barter mentioned by Smith is nowhere to be found. Explorers attempted to find this fabled land but to no avail. If economics is an objective field of study, it is disappointing to know that no economist paid attention to this fact. It is plausible to think that the system of exchange we are using today derived from the story made up by Smith. Instead of barter, researchers discovered diverse processes and systems of exchange among indigenous groups.

Based on studies by scholars, the prehistoric communities in the archipelago engaged in trading within Southeast Asia through barter. From the community level to regional communities, everyone was involved in trading. Are the scholars and academics referring to the double coincidence idea of a barter from the fabled land espoused by Smith? The ideas of barter and debt are very important fields of study for analyzing the social relations of our ancestors. It has been reported that the insubordination of people in prehistoric Tagalog, Visayan, and Kapampangan communities was primarily due to debt that could be passed to children and children's children. Freedom could be regained once the debt was settled. This form of insubordination should not be mistaken for slavery in the West, where human beings owned other human beings.

In the Tagalog context, barangay was a big aggregation of people with established complex social stratification. Datu was the ruling elite. Next to datu was the maharlika class. The warriors, called *bagani*, who were expected to aid the datu in times of peace and war, were recruited from this rank. The bulk of the population consisted of the *timawa* class, or freemen, as described by the early Spanish chroniclers.[13] The lowest rank in the primitive social order was that of the *alipin*, or *oripun* in Visaya. They were the least privileged and consisted of two categories:

1) The *sagigilid* lived in their own houses and served the person they were indebted to. They provided assistance

during the harvest and planting seasons, or when their masters traveled to faraway places. The subordination of the sagigilid was caused by debt, so if they were able to settle their due, they were freed of the obligation to render services.

2) *Namamahay* on the other hand lived with their master in a small hut or makeshift house near the farm. They attended to all kinds of work and had no social privileges at all. Most of them were captured during pangayaw (wars and raids). They could marry only if their master allowed it. Some writers refer to them as slaves, but unlike chattel slaves in the West they could only be sold on rare occasions.

The large population and division of labor explained why trading activities with other Southeast Asian communities could be maintained. It is important to note that the defense carried out by Lapu-Lapu would not have been possible for a small population. As recounted by Antonio Pigafetta,[14] Lapu-Lapu mobilized hundreds of warriors overnight and repulsed Magellan's forces in a low-tide battle along the shores of Mactan, where the cannons from the Spanish ships didn't reach.

Coastal areas around Manila Bay were littered with barangays. Larger barangays were located at the Pasig River's various openings. The finest seaports were in Tondo and Navotas. People traded goods heavily in fragmented patterns. A myriad of unknown barangays participated for a long time. Archeological evidence proved that Sulu, Basilan, and the western part of Mindanao were haven of traders. The movement of *parao* (Indonesian boats) and huge ships back and forth to Sumatra and Java had never stopped since its beginnings in the year 650, before Islam came. After the year 987, *sampan* (Chinese boats) visited the Lingayen Gulf in Pangasinan and the Ilocos region on a regular basis. In the year 1290, parao and sampan started to trade goods along the

Pasig River in Luzon. The trading activities led to the establishment of a *nayon* (big town) called Maynila; across the river was Tondo, a large fishing barangay.

The economic prosperity achieved by Maynila attracted Paduka Sri Sultan Bolkiah,[15] who arrived in 1500 and conquered Maynila twenty years before the Spaniards came. He can be considered the first colonizer—not of the archipelago but of Maynila, which soon became the seat of political power in the republic.

In 1521, Ferdinand Magellan reached Panay, which started the colonization of the archipelago for the kingdom of Spain. Inhuman acts, cruelty, and oppression were perpetuated against the inhabitants in the name of the church and civilization. The entire archipelago was declared to be a part of the territory of Spain, thus establishing centralized government on more than 1,700 islands.

Reflections

Hierarchical relationships are the apex of social problems. A person or group cannot represent the interests of people with very diverse needs and convictions. After the introduction of centralized government, vast numbers of communities and people in the archipelago no longer controlled their own destiny; decisions and policies were made in Spain without any participation from the locals. This setup did not change when the US came and stole the victory from the Katipunan in the name of democracy. The Japanese had their share in the aggression. In the short time of their stay, they inflicted deep misery on the people. Although the US is no longer here physically, their influence, as well as the influence of international institutions, on the central government through the elite group is undeniable.

Ecological crises are just reflections of human relationships based on hierarchy. The privatization of resources and benefit streams cannot be carried out without hierarchical relationships. The accumulation of masses of profit and the control of benefits cannot be realized without exploiting natural resources and human labor.

The existing political structures maintain and reinforce the ownership and control of resources and the economy by the corporations and a few families. This kind of relationship leads people to a dog-eat-dog type behavior. They compete for higher positions for greater incentives and privilege.

The alternatives of state socialists in Russia, China, Cuba, Cambodia, and North Korea failed to install participatory and equitable processes. In many cases, communist parties surpassed in cruelty, slavery, and oppression the previous oppressors of the people they were supposed to liberate. The state socialist and labor parties in Europe also failed to introduce democracy in its real substance.

Why did this happen? It is because hierarchy accumulates privilege. The higher the position in a structure, the greater the access to power and benefits. This promotes competition that makes relationships between people revolve around incentives of privilege and political power. Incentives entice people to produce more for the markets and shops, which results in the massive extraction of natural resources and the exploitation of the earth as a sink, which causes ecological crises. The accumulation of the few "winners" of the competition will eventually lead to poverty and the marginalization of the many.

This pattern can be found in all states in the world, be they welfare, communist, or socialist states. Thus, taking the path toward centralizing political power was an erroneous tactic. The baranganic resistance and primitive communities could have taken advantage of developing their informal ties not through the pattern introduced by the colonizers but through expanding federations of the barangays/communities and through strengthening traditional networks of support and coordination against the oppressors.

Pulling back history is not practical; I believe that humanity recorded it in order to imagine our future. Sure, it is difficult to picture a humane, nonhierarchical, confederal order constructed under the wisdom of indigenous organizations. As human history unfolds, many parts of the earth reveal practical, applicable, and genuinely democratic political processes of decision-making bubbling from below. Some of them were the free assemblies of the Paris Commune of 1871, the early phase of the Russian Revolution, specifically in the Ukraine, Kronstadt, and among the workers of Petrograd. The large-scale application of confederations, free assemblies, and millions of collectives, together with the direct appropriation of anarcho-syndicalist ideas, occurred during the Spanish Civil War of 1936–1937. In Buenos Aires, Argentina, the actual direct management by the workers of two hundred industries took place in 2001; many have survived to this day. The Zapatista experiment offers concrete processes of nonhierarchical and antiauthoritarian alternatives.

These experiences prove that people can be organized not in hierarchical ways but in a horizontal fashion. This means that no individual can exercise authority over others. People come together to cooperate, collaborate, and work in a confederal process in order to meet their needs in an ecologically sustainable, non-oppressive, and equitable manner. We cited foreign experiences not to look for a model but to derive wisdom to enrich our indigenous versions of an anarchist society. We need only turn to our ancestors and current indigenous groups. The anarchist theme subtly passed to us by our ancestors materializes whenever we act directly and without intermediaries on concrete issues, whenever we talk and apply equality and socialism in our circles, whenever we stand for ecological protection, and whenever we send solidarity to the communities of the world who attack hierarchies.

The dominant political relationships in our society are clientelism, patronage, and fantasy politics. The very foundation of these oppressive politics is deeply rooted and has been established through long historical coercive processes of colonization. These made us believe that there are experts who can handle our lives and gave politicians and leaders the power to take care of things that they know nothing about.

The idea of direct democracy is a concrete alternative framework to statist politics and hierarchical relationships. It is mainly associated with Western thought and practice but definitely consistent with our tradition of decentralism, autonomy, and nonhierarchical politics based on cooperation.

To apply this to the archipelago is a great challenge. The privileged class absolutely will never agree to this system, and we do not need to convince them anyway. What we need to do is to retake our own lives from corporations, the state, and other institutions. We do not have to be anarchists embracing propaganda by the deed; we can be anarchists in our everyday lives. We can start at home, attending to household chores, such as laundry, dishwashing, and taking care of our children. Such activities are surely anarchistic in nature, specifically if you do it because you are convinced that you need to partake in housekeeping, because all members of the family should share it.

Production of things we need on a daily basis is another challenge. Corporations provide us with almost all things, but most of them are irrelevant to our daily sustenance. We are trained to work and conditioned to shop and consume. This process actually consumes the world's ecosystems by controlling resources and exploiting people to work in different industries in order to create commodities for shopping. This is designed to achieve limitless growth.

Alternatives should be doable at home, because if it will not work in our own household, we do not have the basis to encourage people to adopt alternatives. Techniques in gardening to maximize space which promotes chemical-free vegetables has been proven effective by many infoshops and collectives in the archipelago. Adopting renewable energy technology increases our independence from greedy power corporations. Creating independent spaces for recreation and learning at the community level will increase solidarity and participation of the people within our community. There are plenty of things we can experiment with and explore; groups as well as individuals can engage in activities that encourage autonomy.

We can replicate this at the community level by initiating nonhierarchical activities that can directly contribute to addressing concrete manifestations of oppression. For instance, organizing one-time feeding activities (Food not Bombs) is not appealing for the mainstream political parties. Providing foods for the homeless collected from luxurious gatherings for instance is a direct action that confronts hunger. Organizing a feeding activity for a tiny fraction of hundreds of thousand hungry people can concretely deliver results, more concrete than organizing a mobilization to publicize demands. The question of sustainability is indeed a critical concern, but we should be reminded that we are not the solution to hunger but, rather, contributors to realize food security.

We cannot change the world by providing food alone, but as long as we handle things directly to achieve particular objectives without any intermediaries, we contribute to the critique against the machineries of hierarchy. Propaganda is inherent in every action. If an individual or a collective successfully meet their objectives, this will definitely send messages to their immediate environments. The public probably will be first surprised to learn that the annoying-looking kids are providing food for the homeless and organize art workshops for poor communities, but they will soon realize that they can do the same to support their marginalized peers.

Avenues that encourage people's meaningful participation in decision-making are crucial. Meaningful participation will not be possible in a republican and representative setup. Education is key to address bossism, clientelism, dependency, and ignorance. People will be more active and critical if they have information and appropriate venues.

Direct democracy will allow us to explore processes that are liberatory and participatory—a critical component in shifting power relations from centralization to power-sharing.

Anarchy

I intentionally placed anarchy last because the anarchist framework can summarize major points and assertions of this text. Anarchism is a political idea invented by people not out of abstraction. It was developed through actual interaction of the people among themselves and with ecological systems, and it can be traced during prehistoric times. Anarchist practices are diverse, based on the multitude, and they have a myriad of variations. Despite the diversity, there are characteristics common among these anarchist practices, such as solidarity, decentralization, mutual aid, noncoerciveness, anti-patriarchy, direct action, and ecologically sound ways of living. Thousand years before Europeans coined the word *anarchism*, it was already practiced by myriad indigenous communities in many places around the world. In fact, the traditional social relations of our ancestors were anarchistic, and the remaining indigenous communities up to the present day are still practicing such cultures and lifeways.

Social revolution is indeed a process that will educate the people about the evil of the state; it is a process that will abolish hierarchy to regain self-determination. Political revolution in many instances mentioned above is a hindrance to social revolution.

Acknowledgments

I would like to extend my gratitude to the following collectives and individuals for their contributions and direct as well as indirect influence on the development of this essay. I am truly honored that I am not denied support by the following. . .

Food Not Bomb crews: Cainta, Makati, Lucena, Baliwag Bulacan, Cavite, Cebu City.

Collectives: Anarchist Initiative for Direct-Democracy (AID collective), NON-Collective, Pinagkaisahan collective (Bulacan), As a Whole Family (Davao), Samcore (Sampaloc), Anti-Panis, Mobile Anarchist School, Mutual Aid Not Charity (Sapang-Palay Bulacan), Ferral Crust, Flower Grave, Notra Block, Mag-Isa Collective, Organic Minds, Maharlika Integral, Theo sa Kanto.

Infoshops: Manila Infoshop, Etniko Bandido, Flying House/ Tarima, Balay-Likhaan Tuklasan, Bee Hive Collective, Safehouse Infoshop, Irregular Rhythm Asylum.

Campaigns/Projects/Network: Sagada 11, Local Autnomous Network, Sining Kalikasan Aklasan (SKA).

Individuals: Ramon Fernando, Randy Nobleza, Rodney, Ronald (Beauty of Doubt), Jong Pairez, Kristek, Boy Dada, Fritz, Pepe Tanchuling, Ted Jacinto, Bong Escober, Lito Anunuevo, Bob Black, Gabriel Kuhn, Kaori, Kim Hill, Chris French, Maxx Ourg, Bram Sickos, Pintig-Yaman, Keith Mc Henry, Mark and Terry, Gary Granada.

My immediate collective is my family. They provide most of the assistance I need.
Sa gabay ng ating mga ninuno. . .

NOTES

1   Based on his study of the history of humankind, Peter Kropotkin described how the practice of mutual aid allowed people to improve and develop their knowledge, culture, and human intelligence. In addition, cooperation was based on the premise that only the fittest survive, not individually but as a species.
2   Waziyatawin and Michael Yellow Bird, eds., "Introduction," in *For Indigenous Minds Only: A Decolonization Handbook* (Santa Fe: School of Advanced Research Press, 2012), 3.
3   "Fourth Quarter 2014 Social Weather Survey: Hunger Falls to 17.2% of families; Moderate Hunger 13.2%, Severe Hunger 4.1%," Social Weather Stations, January 26, 2015, www.sws.org.ph/swsmain/artc ldisppage/?artcsyscode=ART-20151122001030.
4   See page 51, note 8.
5   Joyce C. White, "Incorporating Heterarchy into Theory on Socio political Development: The Case from Southeast Asia," *Archeological Papers of the American Anthropological Association* 6, no. 1 (January 1995): 101–23.
6   The Treaty of Tordesillas, signed in 1494, divided the lands colonized by Portugal and Spain between them.—editor's note
7   Waziyatawin and Yellow Bird, "Introduction," 2–3.
8   Ibid., 8.

9   The term *datu* refers to traditional leaders in the archipelago later known as the Philippines.

10   Emma Helen Blair and James Alexander Robertson, *The Philippine Islands, 1493–1898, Volume XXIII, 1629–30*, Project Gutenberg, www.gutenberg.org/files/16451/16451-h/16451-h.htm.

11   An *encomendero* was equipped with an *encomienda* and ruled over subjects, mostly indigenous people, whose labor he could exploit at will.—editor's note

12   David Graeber, *Debt: The First 5,000 Years* (New York: Melville House, 2011), chapter 2, "The Myth of Barter," 21–41.

13   They served the datu and maharlika, and in return they received economic assistance and protection in times of danger.

14   See page 50, note 6.

15   From 1485 to 1524, Paduka Sri Sultan Bolkiah was the king of Brunei, a rich town on the island of Borneo.

RESOURCES

Benedict Anderson's 2005 book *Under Three Flags: Anarchism and the Anti-Colonial Imagination*, referenced and cited several times in this book, is the classic study of anarchist influence on political thought and action in the Philippines and remains easily available.

In 2016, the Mobile Anarchist School edited a book titled *Anarchist Feminists in the Philippines*. It can be ordered from the Etniko Bandido infoshop (etnikobandidoinfoshop.wordpress.com) or from Active Distribution (www.activedistributionshop.org).

There are some very useful texts in English about anarchism in the Philippines to be found online:

Loma Cuevas-Hewitt's 2016 doctoral thesis *Re-Imagined Communities: The Radical Imagination from Philippine Independence to the Postcolonial Presence* includes a 50-page chapter on "The Anarchists." It can be downloaded at api.research-repository.uwa.edu.au/portalfiles/portal/9794911/THESIS_DOCTOR_OF_PHILOSOPHY_CUEVAS_HEWITT_Marco_2016.pdf.[1]

Portia Ladrido's article "The Anarchists Making a Difference in Philippine Society" is at cnnphilippines.com/life/culture/2017/09/06/anarchists-making-a-difference-in-Philippine-society.html.

The Anarchist Zine Library contains a PDF folder about "Anarchism, History and Movement in the Philippines," available at azinelibrary.org/approved/anarchism-philippines.pdf.

A 2012 call for support by the publishing project Mindsetbreaker Press also includes first-hand information about the anarchist movement in the Philippines. It is archived at uncomradelybehaviour.wordpress.com/2012/ 04/28/anarchism-in-the philippines and 325.nostate.net/ 2012/04/12/anarchist-call-for-support-from-mindsetbreaker-press-distro-philippines.

Plenty of English-language material is available on the website of the Bandilang Itim collective (bandilangitim. noblogs.org), including PDFs of their self-titled zine and the *Gasera* journal.

In 2015, the Final Straw radio podcast on Asheville FM released an interview with members of the Maharlika Integral Emergence (MIE) collective from Davao. The archive page also contains links to further information: thefinalstrawradio. noblogs.org/post/2015/07/20/anarchy-in-davao-maharlika-so-called-philippines-a-chat-with-members-of-the-mie-collective.

Albeit not focused on political activism, the 2018 Dazed short film documentary "Anarchy in the Philippines" provides an insight into punk culture in the Philippines, which often overlaps with anarchist culture. At the time of writing, the film was accessible for free online.

Also titled "Anarchy in the Philippines" and produced by radical-guide.com, a 2018 online interview with Cris from Etniko Bandido Infoshop was also accessible online for free at the time of writing.

Regular updates on anarchist activities in the Philippines can be found at etnikobandidoinfoshop.wordpress.com.

NOTES

1   See page 11, note 2 about Cuevas-Hewitt's name change.

ABOUT THE CONTRIBUTORS

Bas Umali is a longtime organizer living in Metro Manila. He has been involved with digital and physical infoshops, mobile education initiatives, climate crises campaigns, natural disaster relief programs, and bringing solar technology to marginalized communities. Bas has worked for an NGO concerned with rainforest rehabilitation and driven Grab and Uber vehicles. Today, he provides technical assistance to marginalized fisherfolk and dreams of settling in the countryside with his family.

Jong Pairez is an independent cultural researcher and media artist based in Tokyo. He holds degrees from the University of the Philippines College of Fine Arts and the Tokyo University of the Arts. Jong is the founder of Civilisation Laboratory (CIV:LAB), a tactical space dedicated to research and design of sustainable and alternative living, and considers himself a foreign migrant worker in the lost-decade generation.

Loma Cuevas-Hewitt earned a Ph.D. in Cultural Anthropology from the University of Western Australia, and since then has been working as a researcher in a range of not-for-profits and consultancies. Based in Sydney, Australia, Loma is also an environmental justice activist and aspiring prose poet.

Gabriel Kuhn is an independent author and translator living in Sweden. Among his titles with PM Press are *Turning Money into Rebellion: The Unlikely Story of Denmark's Revolutionary Bank Robbers* (2014) and *Liberating Sápmi: Indigenous Resistance in Europe's Far North* (2020).

ABOUT PM PRESS

PM Press is an independent, radical publisher of books and media to educate, entertain, and inspire. Founded in 2007 by a small group of people with decades of publishing, media, and organizing experience, PM Press amplifies the voices of radical authors, artists, and activists. Our aim is to deliver bold political ideas and vital stories to all walks of life and arm the dreamers to demand the impossible. We have sold millions of copies of our books, most often one at a time, face to face. We're old enough to know what we're doing and young enough to know what's at stake. Join us to create a better world.

PM Press
PO Box 23912
Oakland, CA 94623
www.pmpress.org

PM Press in Europe
europe@pmpress.org
www.pmpress.org.uk

FRIENDS OF PM PRESS

These are indisputably momentous times—the financial system is melting down globally and the Empire is stumbling. Now more than ever there is a vital need for radical ideas.

In the years since its founding—and on a mere shoestring—PM Press has risen to the formidable challenge of publishing and distributing knowledge and entertainment for the struggles ahead. With over 450 releases to date, we have published an impressive and stimulating array of literature, art, music, politics, and culture. Using every available medium, we've succeeded in connecting those hungry for ideas and information to those putting them into practice.

Friends of PM allows you to directly help impact, amplify, and revitalize the discourse and actions of radical writers, filmmakers, and artists. It provides us with a stable foundation from which we can build upon our early successes and provides a much-needed subsidy for the materials that can't necessarily pay their own way. You can help make that happen—and receive every new title automatically delivered to your door once a month—by joining as a Friend of PM Press. And, we'll throw in a free T-shirt when you sign up.

Here are your options:

- **$30 a month** Get all books and pamphlets plus 50% discount on all webstore purchases

- **$40 a month** Get all PM Press releases (including CDs and DVDs) plus 50% discount on all webstore purchases

- **$100 a month** Superstar—Everything plus PM merchandise, free downloads, and 50% discount on all webstore purchases

For those who can't afford $30 or more a month, we have **Sustainer Rates** at $15, $10 and $5. Sustainers get a free PM Press T-shirt and a 50% discount on all purchases from our website.

Your Visa or Mastercard will be billed once a month, until you tell us to stop. Or until our efforts succeed in bringing the revolution around. Or the financial meltdown of Capital makes plastic redundant. Whichever comes first.

Liberating Sápmi: Indigenous Resistance in Europe's Far North

Gabriel Kuhn

ISBN: 978-1-62963-712-9
$17.00   220 pages

The Sámi, who have inhabited Europe's far north for thousands of years, are often referred to as the continent's "forgotten people." With Sápmi, their traditional homeland, divided between four nation-states—Norway, Sweden, Finland, and Russia—the Sámi have experienced the profound oppression and discrimination that characterize the fate of indigenous people worldwide: their lands have been confiscated, their beliefs and values attacked, their communities and families torn apart. Yet the Sámi have shown incredible resilience, defending their identity and their territories and retaining an important social and ecological voice—even if many, progressives and leftists included, refuse to listen.

Liberating Sápmi is a stunning journey through Sápmi and includes in-depth interviews with Sámi artists, activists, and scholars boldly standing up for the rights of their people. In this beautifully illustrated work, Gabriel Kuhn, author of over a dozen books and our most fascinating interpreter of global social justice movements, aims to raise awareness of the ongoing fight of the Sámi for justice and self-determination. The first accessible English-language introduction to the history of the Sámi people and the first account that focuses on their political resistance, this provocative work gives irrefutable evidence of the important role the Sámi play in the resistance of indigenous people against an economic and political system whose power to destroy all life on earth has reached a scale unprecedented in the history of humanity.

The book contains interviews with Mari Boine, Harald Gaski, Ann-Kristin Håkansson, Aslak Holmberg, Maxida Märak, Stefan Mikaelsson, May-Britt Öhman, Synnøve Persen, Øyvind Ravna, Niillas Somby, Anders Sunna, and Suvi West.

"I'm highly recommending Gabriel Kuhn's book Liberating Sápmi *to anyone seeking to understand the world of today through indigenous eyes. Kuhn concisely and dramatically opens our eyes to little-known Sápmi history, then in the perfect follow-up brings us up to date with a unique collection of interviews with a dozen of today's most brilliant contemporary Sámi voices. Bravo."*
—Buffy Sainte-Marie, Cree, singer-songwriter

X: Straight Edge and Radical Sobriety

Gabriel Kuhn

ISBN: 978-1-62963-716-7
$22.95   352 pages

Straight edge—hardcore punk's drug-free offshoot—has thrived as a subculture since the early 1980s. Its influence has reached far beyond musical genres and subcultural divides. Today it is more diverse and richly complex than ever, and in the past decade alcohol and drug use have become a much-discussed issue in radical politics, not least due to the hard work, dedication, and commitment to social and environmental justice found among straight-edge activists.

X: Straight Edge and Radical Sobriety is Gabriel Kuhn's highly anticipated follow-up to his critically acclaimed *Sober Living for the Revolution*. In this impressive volume, Kuhn continues his reconnaissance of straight-edge culture and how it overlaps with radical politics. Extensively illustrated and combining original interviews and essays with manifestos and reprints from zines and pamphlets, *X* is a vital portrait of the wide spectrum of people who define straight-edge culture today.

In the sprawling scope of this book, the notion of straight edge as a bastion of white, middle-class, cis males is openly confronted and boldly challenged by dozens of contributors who span five continents. *X* takes a piercing look at religion, identity, feminism, aesthetics, harm reduction, and much more. It is both a call to action and an elaborate redefinition of straight edge and radical sobriety.

Promising to inspire discussion, reflection, and unearth hidden chapters of hardcore punk history, *X: Straight Edge and Radical Sobriety* is of crucial importance to anybody interested in the politics of punk and social transformation.

"Straight-edge culture is very diverse, and parts of it always had a strong emphasis on emancipation and equality, also with regard to gender and sexuality. It's good to have a book acknowledging this."
—Jenni Ramme, Emancypunx Records

"Forget the clichés—straight edge isn't just about buff white dudes. Kuhn's book shows that it's a multifaceted social movement rooted in the intersection of DIY culture and political resistance."
—Lori Black Bear, Sprout Distro

A Soldier's Story: Revolutionary Writings by a New Afrikan Anarchist, Third Edition

Kuwasi Balagoon, edited by Matt Meyer and Karl Kersplebedeb

ISBN: 978-1-62963-377-0
$19.95   272 pages

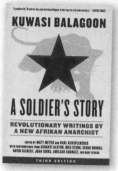

Kuwasi Balagoon was a participant in the Black Liberation struggle from the 1960s until his death in prison in 1986. A member of the Black Panther Party and defendant in the infamous Panther 21 case, Balagoon went underground with the Black Liberation Army (BLA). Captured and convicted of various crimes against the State, he spent much of the 1970s in prison, escaping twice. After each escape, he went underground and resumed BLA activity.

Balagoon was unusual for his time in several ways. He combined anarchism with Black nationalism, he broke the rules of sexual and political conformity that surrounded him, he took up arms against the white-supremacist state—all the while never shying away from developing his own criticisms of the weaknesses within the movements. His eloquent trial statements and political writings, as much as his poetry and excerpts from his prison letters, are all testimony to a sharp and iconoclastic revolutionary who was willing to make hard choices and fully accept the consequences.

Balagoon was captured for the last time in December 1981, charged with participating in an armored truck expropriation in West Nyack, New York, an action in which two police officers and a money courier were killed. Convicted and sentenced to life imprisonment, he died of an AIDS-related illness on December 13, 1986.

The first part of this book consists of contributions by those who knew or were touched by Balagoon. The second section consists of court statements and essays by Balagoon himself, including several documents that were absent from previous editions and have never been published before. The third consists of excerpts from letters Balagoon wrote from prison. A final fourth section consists of a historical essay by Akinyele Umoja and an extensive intergenerational roundtable discussion of the significance of Balagoon's life and thoughts today.